Carry-Along
CROCHET

By Leslie Linsley

Sedgewood® Press
New York, NY

Craft Contributors:

Anna Beck

Robin Marie Murray

Judy Ann DeFelippis

Lori Scamporino

Sally George

Mary F. Smith

Anne Lane

Roberta Sohmer

Ruth Linsley

Projects on pages 53, 77, 119, and 162 were designed by Anne Lane
Projects on pages 134 and 139 were designed by Sally George
Projects on pages 154 and 158 were designed by Mary F. Smith

Robin Murray deserves special thanks for her participation throughout the writing of the book. Her design and instructional input are always invaluable.

I would like to extend my appreciation to the yarn manufacturers and distributors who have been helpful in the preparation of the book. They are:

Bernat Yarn and Craft Co.
Uxbridge, MA

Phildar, Inc.
Norcross, GA

Caron International Inc.
Rochelle, IL

Tahki Imports Ltd.
Hackensack, NJ

Coats & Clark, Inc.
Stamford, CT

William Unger & Co. Inc.
New York, NY

For Sedgewood® Press
Editorial Director: Elizabeth P. Rice
Project Editor: Susan Gies
Associate Editor: Leslie Gilbert
Production Manager: Bill Rose
Design: Remo Cosentino
Photography: Thomas Famighetti

Distributed by Macmillan Publishing Company, a division of Macmillan, Inc.

ISBN 0-02-496760-2
Library of Congress Catalog Card Number: 84-52786

Printed in the United States of America

Contents

Introduction

Crochet is a French word meaning "little hook." The craft of crochet dates back to sixteenth century Italy, where it began; later, crochet spread to Spain and then to Ireland. In England, after Queen Victoria was given a gift of crochet-edged table linens, crochet quickly became the rage in high society. Suitors brought crocheted gifts to win the hearts of young women, and it was unthinkable to christen a baby in anything but a crocheted dress.

Crochet reached America in the nineteenth and early twentieth centuries through a magazine: *Godey's Lady's Book.* Once they took to it, American women began to create new designs, fashioning flowers, stars, pineapples, and appliqué patterns that were familiar in the world of quilting. These patterns and designs, created in the early part of this century, are as beautifully at home with decorating styles today as they were with those of earlier times.

When I wrote my first book of crochet projects, it was in response to a revived awareness of the craft. My research showed me that crocheting has been part of women's lives for centuries—mothers teach their daughters, who teach their own daughters, and so on. This craft has provided a pleasant and practical pastime for generations.

While our ancestors had the time to create painstakingly crocheted tablecloths, afghans, shawls, and edgings for linens, today's crafters have precious little time for such exquisite, finely detailed projects. But many of us do enjoy handwork for the satisfaction this craft brings.

Carry-Along Crochet responds to the desire for such satisfaction as well as to an ever-increasing need for portable crochet projects. Most of us are on the go for part of the day; if a project is portable, it can be done during odd moments of waiting or during otherwise wasted time. Many of us travel or commute to work. A carry-along project can fit into a purse or tote bag and can be comfortably worked on a bus, train or subway. These projects are small or—in the case of an afghan—can be made in pieces. They do not require any setting up, so they can be worked in small increments of time. Carry-along projects are ideal for crafters who enjoy doing their handwork while relaxing in front of the television or sitting and socializing.

Many carry-along projects are small, but they are by no means insignificant. A pair of booties for that newborn baby, a soft mohair cap for a winter's day, a Little Red Riding Hood toy for a toddler—these are a few of the projects that make up this book. As a craft writer, designer, and do-it-yourselfer of many years, I've collected letters and suggestions from readers all over the country. They tell me about new projects they would like to see as well as how old favorites can be adapted to meet the needs of a changing lifestyle. For example, Roberta, the crocheter who made the afghan on page 44, works full time at a police station. It's a hectic job, so for relaxation she likes to keep a crochet project or two going at all times. "I pick it up whenever I have a free moment. It relaxes me," says Roberta. Many crafters are like Roberta; they juggle full-time jobs, children, and many other activities. Still, they like to make things for themselves, their homes, and to give as gifts. That hasn't changed; what has changed—a great deal—are the kinds of projects that interest most people. Crocheters tell me again and again to keep the projects simple. One woman attends many meetings and says she will only work on a lap project. "I don't mind doing the finishing work at home, but I carry my crafting wherever I go. If it doesn't fit in my purse or tote bag, I can't be bothered to make it."

All of us want to have nice things in our homes, but often we can't afford them. This is one of the best reasons for making handcrafted items ourselves. So while a crafted project might be easy to do and portable, we also want it to be as good-looking as something we would buy. Our time is worth a lot to us and we need to know that we've spent it wisely.

The letters that I receive suggest ideas for new designs and projects. These ideas help me dream up the items that I think people want to make the most. Many of the projects are familiar; my challenge is to design them in a new way so that they will be exciting to make.

For this book I took many familiar items and redesigned them to be portable. For example, the sweaters on pages 56 and 74 are designed so that each section can be completed individually and then stitched together once you have the time at home to finish the project. The popular ripple pattern is used for our commuter afghan. However, it has been created from strips that are later joined to form the whole. There are many granny square afghans, but I think you'll find them more interesting than ordinary. The daisy afghan on page 106, for example, is a familiar pattern often found in large squares of yellow on a green background and made for an adult-size bed. This time I made small squares of yellow and white on a baby-blue background for a delicate carriage blanket. The work is quick and easy, pretty and portable.

The lacy afghan on page 34 is done in ecru wool. It is as soft and elegant as any blanket can be and the pattern, while familiar, is always popular and a guaranteed decorating success. The design complements any furnishing style and it is easy to add squares if needed to fit a larger bed size. This project makes a wonderful wedding present, one that will be cherished for a lifetime.

Some projects take more time than others, but are worth the extra effort. These projects often don't look as time-consuming as they are. Such is the case with the lovely filet crochet edgings. The stitches for this work form a delicate, lacy web, interrupted by solid stitches at evenly spaced intervals; the stitches form a design motif. To make a large tablecloth, for example, would be quite an undertaking. As an edging, however, this form of crochet is easy to do and can be added to any piece of fabric. Traditionally done on very small hooks and using very fine thread, a filet crochet project might well take several months to make. I have redesigned some of the old, beautiful patterns so that you use a slightly larger hook and heavier thread. In this way the pattern can be duplicated in much less time than it would have taken originally.

You can usually judge by the size of the hook and the weight of the yarn whether a project will take more or less time than another. A project made with a large hook and heavy yarn takes far less time to complete than one made with a small hook and fine yarn. With a project that might otherwise be difficult, I have, whenever possible, devised a method for creating the item so that the results are as beautiful, but the time spent has been altered for more care-free crafting.

People who are doing craftwork come from all over the country and represent a diversified group. They are ardent craftworkers, but not necessarily experts at all crafts. In fact, many of the readers who contact me are new to a particular craft and often make suggestions for future books. Through this informal network, I can continue to research and present crafting techniques in high-interest areas.

I especially enjoy the anecdotes that accompany almost every crafting experience that readers write about. Animals and babies seem to be the greatest cause for distraction at crucial crafting moments. One woman has a telephone answering machine that simply says, "Call me later, I'm in the middle of a complicated stitch." She says her friends are very understanding.

And so it is that this selection of carry-along crochet projects came about. Portable projects are perfect for our busy lifestyles. Quick and easy directions make it possible to finish a project before you lose interest or before a child grows too much to fit into the sweater you started for him or her. But best of all I think you'll be pleased with results of your handwork. There is a nice variety of home accessories, clothing, toys, and gifts presented here.

Should you feel like jotting down a note about your experiences or suggestions please send it along to me. In this way we can continue to share in the crafting experience.

Leslie Linsley

Getting Started in Crochet

Most of the projects made in crochet can be achieved with a few basic stitches. All the work starts with a chain made up of a series of loops on a crochet hook. Unlike knitting, which is done on 2, 3, and sometimes 4 needles, crocheting is done on a single hook. Hooks come in various sizes. The size you use will depend on the yarn, pattern, and item you are crocheting.

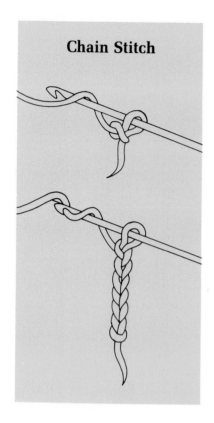

Chain Stitch

CHAIN STITCH (CH)

All projects in this book begin with a foundation of the chain stitch.

1. Make a slip knot by taking yarn about 2 inches from end and winding it once around your middle 3 fingers.

2. Pull a length of yarn through the loop around your fingers. Put this new loop on your crochet hook and pull tight.

3. With yarn wound over left-hand fingers, pass the hook under the yarn on your index finger and catch a strand with the hook.

4. Draw the yarn through the loop already on the hook to make one chain stitch. Repeat Steps 3 and 4 for as many chain stitches as needed. If you hold the chain as close to the hook as possible with the thumb and index finger of your left hand, the chain will be even.

The beginning of every project in crochet is a row of a specific number of chain stitches. These are the basis of the piece, just as the cast-on row is the basis of a knit piece.

At the beginning of every row an extra chain stitch is made. This is counted as the first stitch of the row and is called "the turning chain."

SINGLE CROCHET (SC)

Make a foundation chain.

1. Insert hook in 2nd chain from the hook (the skipped chain is the turning chain) and bring the yarn over the hook from back to front (clockwise). Pull the yarn over through the chain so you have 2 loops on the hook. (*Note*: In these instructions, each chain stitch is simply called a "chain." Where a string of chain stitches is being discussed, it is known by the numbers of stitches; for example, "first chain-5" means the first group of 5 chain stitches in a row.)

2. Wind the yarn around the hook again and draw the hook with its 3rd loop through the 2 loops already on the hook. You have made a single crochet (sc).

3. Continue to work a single crochet in each chain stitch. At the end of the row, make 1 chain and turn your work around from right to left so that the reverse is facing you.

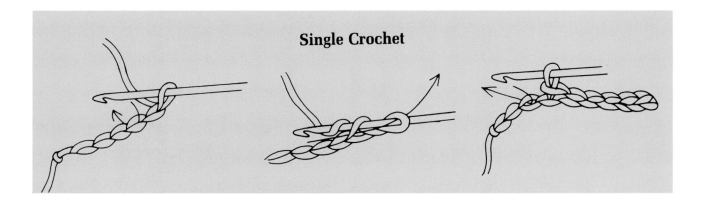

Single Crochet

4. The turning chain stitch counts as the first stitch for the next row. Work the next single crochet by inserting your hook through the top loop of the next stitch from the previous row. Wind the yarn over the hook (yo) and draw it through the stitch. Yarn over and through 2 loops on hook. Continue to work a single crochet stitch across row. Chain 1 and turn.

FASTENING OFF
At the end of all required rows or rounds, cut the yarn with a tail of 2 or 3 inches and draw it through the last loop at the end of the row. Pull tightly and weave it into the fabric with a yarn needle. Sometimes the tail is used to sew pieces together. Cut off yarn according to how the piece will be used. Sometimes you may need more to sew with.

DOUBLE CROCHET (DC)
Make a foundation chain.

1. Yarn over hook and insert hook in 4th chain from hook.

2. Yarn over hook. Draw through chain. There are 3 loops on hook.

3. Yarn over hook. Draw through 2 loops on hook. There are now 2 loops on hook.

4. Yarn over hook. Draw yarn through the last 2 loops on hook. One double crochet (dc) is completed. Insert hook into the next stitch in foundation chain and repeat Steps 2, 3, and 4.

Once you've worked a double crochet in every chain across the

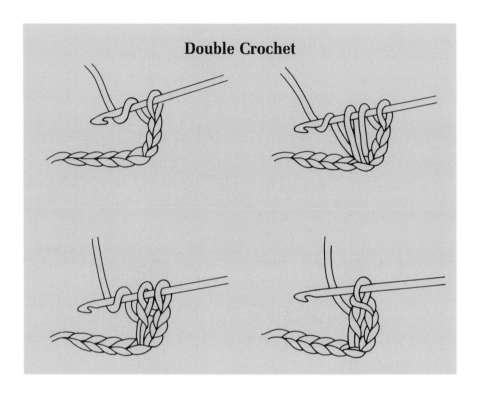

Double Crochet

row, chain 3 and turn. This turning chain of 3 chain stitches counts as 1 double crochet beginning the next row.

5. Skip the first stitch and work a double crochet in the top loop of each double crochet across.

6. Work a double crochet in the first stitches of the chain-3 (turning chain).

HALF DOUBLE CROCHET (HDC)

Make a foundation chain.

1. Yarn over hook and insert hook through loop of 3rd chain from hook.

2. Yarn over hook. Draw yarn through the chain so there are 3 loops on hook.

3. Yarn over hook. Draw through all 3 loops to complete half double crochet (hdc).

Half Double Crochet

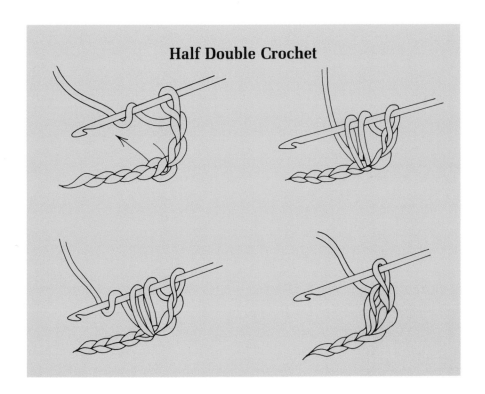

Continue to do this in each chain across row. At the end of the row, chain 2 to turn. Skip the first stitch and work first half double crochet into each half double crochet across. The last half double crochet in the row is worked in the turning chain. Chain 2 to turn.

TREBLE CROCHET (TR)

Make a foundation chain.

1. With 1 loop on your hook, put the yarn over the hook twice. Insert hook in the 5th chain from the hook, yarn over hook and pull the loop through. Bring the yarn over the hook, draw it through 2 loops at once, 3 times.

2. Yarn over hook, pull yarn through the 2 loops on your hook 2 more times. There will be 1 loop on the hook which completes the treble (sometimes called triple) crochet.

3. Bring yarn over the hook twice. Insert the hook into the next chain. Repeat by bringing the yarn over the hook; pull through.

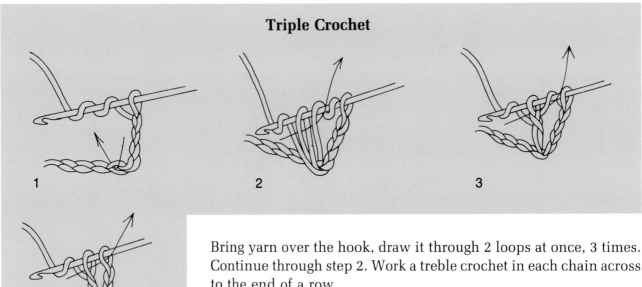

Triple Crochet

1 2 3

4

5

Bring yarn over the hook, draw it through 2 loops at once, 3 times. Continue through step 2. Work a treble crochet in each chain across to the end of a row.

4. At the end of the row, chain 4 and turn. This turning chain of 4 is the first treble crochet of the next row. The last treble of the row is worked in the fourth turning chain of the previous row.

DOUBLE TREBLE CROCHET (DTR)
Make a foundation chain.

With 1 loop on your hook, put the yarn over the hook 3 times. Insert hook into the sixth chain of your foundation chain. Pull the loop through. Yarn over, draw through 2 loops at once. Repeat 3 times more.

TURNING
Depending on the crochet stitch you are working, you will need a number of chain stitches at the end of each row. For a single crochet, you will chain 2; for a double crochet, chain 3; for a treble crochet, chain 4.

SLIP STITCH (SL ST)
A slip stitch is used to join chains in order to form a ring. Insert the hook into the chain. Yarn over hook and draw through both stitch and loop on hook in one motion. This completes 1 slip stitch (sl st).

JOINING ROUNDS

If you are making a hat, for example, work to the end of the round, according to directions given for the specific project. Then join by inserting hook into the top loop of the first stitch on the same round you have been working, and work a slip stitch. In this way you join the first and last stitches of the round.

WORKING IN SPACES

In crocheted work that is lacy and contains openwork, often you are instructed to skip over a stitch in the preceding row and to chain across the gap. Sometimes, too, your pattern will ask you to work stitches in a space, rather than a stitch. In that case, insert your hook through the gap, or space (sp), rather than through a stitch in the preceding row. Often, as a way of increasing stitches, several stitches are worked in 1 space.

AFGHAN STITCH

The afghan stitch is often used as a background over which cross-stitch or embroidery is added. Begin with a crocheted chain of the desired length.

Row 1: Beginning in the 2nd chain, draw up a loop in each stitch of the chain, leaving all loops on the hook. Work off loops as follows: Yarn over hook, draw through 1 loop, * yarn over hook, draw through 2 loops, repeat from * across the row leaving 1 loop on the hook.

Row 2: Skip the first upright bar and draw up a loop in each upright bar, leaving all loops on the hook. Work off loops in the way you did in Row 1.

Repeat Row 2 for the specified length given in directions for item to be made.

PICOT

A picot stitch is often used as a decoration made at intervals on an edging. This is done while doing single crochet or slip stitch. Chain the required number of stitches, single crochet or slip stitch in the top stitch of the edge. Repeat across, spacing as per the instructions.

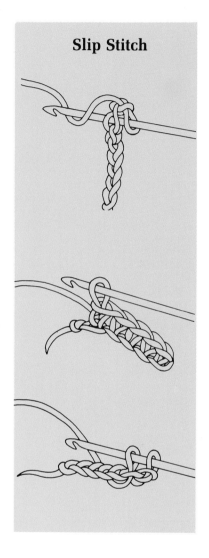

Slip Stitch

Decrease Single Crochet

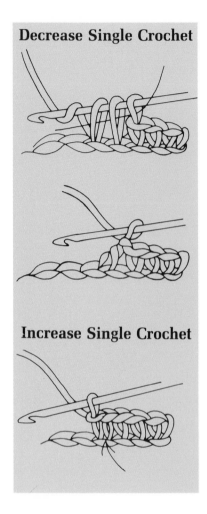

Increase Single Crochet

INCREASING SINGLE CROCHET

When a pattern calls for an increase of a single crochet, work 2 stitches in 1 stitch.

DECREASING SINGLE CROCHET

When a pattern calls for a decrease of a single crochet, pull up a loop in 1 stitch, then pull up a loop in the next stitch, so that there are 3 loops on your hook. Yarn over hook and draw through all 3 loops at once.

YARNS

Most yarns used for knitting can also be used for crochet projects. However, the very fine crochet cotton will enable you to achieve a lacy motif that is more delicate than the effect created with traditional knitting yarns.

   As is true for knitting, it is best to buy the total amount of yarn you will need to finish a project. Check the number printed on the yarn label to be sure that all of the yarn is from the same dye lot. Often the colors change slightly from one dye lot to another, and, if you run out in the middle of a project, you may not be able to find the exact yarn to finish.

CHOOSING YARN

While I've indicated the best yarn for the projects in this book, you should know something about selecting yarns for future projects. Most yarns fit into these categories:

Knitting Worsted

A commonly used yarn that is usually 4-ply. It is a heavy, every-day-type yarn, usually of man-made fibers.

Sport Weight Yarn

Another everyday yarn, it can be 3-ply or 4-ply and is relatively inexpensive. Also made of man-made fibers, it is about half the weight of knitting worsted.

Fingering or Baby Yarns

These are usually thin and soft and require a small hook. They are used mostly for small projects, as it would take a long time to make a larger project with baby yarn.

Bulky Yarns

These are very heavy and are often used to make outdoor sweaters. This type of yarn is worked on large hooks. There is usually a good selection of interesting hand spun and imported bulky yarns.

Wool

Wool comes in many weights and colors. Most crafters like to work with wool the best, as it is pleasant to feel when you are holding it for stretches of time. It is, perhaps, the warmest of all the yarns, but it requires a bit more care than do the synthetics. It must be stored properly and requires blocking. Always save the label for instructions after your project has been completed.

Cotton

Cotton is wonderful for items that will be washed often, such as place mats, pot holders, and baby garments. There are a variety of colors available and cotton is often less expensive than most other yarns.

Acrylic

Acrylic is the most popular of yarns. It is easy to find in almost any color desired, it is washable, it will not shrink, and it is inexpensive. This yarn is used most often for children's clothes, baby afghans, and very large items for which cost is a factor.

If you choose to use a yarn of a different weight than the one I have recommended for a given project you must realize that the amount of yarn you will need to complete the project may change drastically. That is not to say that you shouldn't experiment, but I suggest that you bring the pattern to your yarn store and discuss the changes you desire with the salesperson. She should be able to help you buy the right amount of yarn, and the appropriate hook for the yarn you choose.

GAUGE

A gauge is always given when the size is important. This is always true with a garment or an afghan that is being made to fit a specific bed size, for example. However, many of the projects in this book do not require a gauge, such as toys, Christmas ornaments, and some of the blankets. As long as you use the recommended yarn and hook size, your project will not be so far from the original size to make a difference in the finished item.

If a gauge *is* given at the beginning of a project it is important to check it. The following will be helpful:

Make a swatch approximately 4 by 4 inches, using the yarn, hook, and stitch pattern recommended. This will give you a chance to see the yarn made up, as well as to check the gauge before beginning the project. Count the recommended stitches for the given inches and mark with pins at the beginning and end. With a tape measure on the flat swatch, check to see if they correspond. If you have fewer stitches per inch than the pattern calls for, your work is too loose. Change to a smaller hook. If the stitches measure more than they should, then go up one hook size. Make another swatch to be sure the gauge is correct and adjust accordingly.

TYPES OF HOOKS

Crochet is done with the simple hook made especially for this purpose. The size of the hook determines the size of the stitch.

Hooks come in many different sizes and each is given a number or letter. Some hooks are made of plastic, steel, aluminum, or wood. You can buy the individual size you need for a specific project or a set containing a variety of the most used sizes.

Aluminum hooks are the most popular and easiest to use. They are smooth and lightweight and come in all sizes for all different projects. The very fine filet crochet work, for example, is done with a steel hook that can be found in the smallest sizes.

Very heavy yarn or rope used to make large stitches and bulky projects is often worked on a large plastic hook. Wooden hooks are less common, as they are not durable.

Aluminum hooks are indicated by letters. A K size hook, for example, is quite large, while a D size hook is much smaller. Steel hooks are indicated by numbers. A size 14 steel hook is extremely tiny, while a size 0 is much larger. The hook size is a clue to the type of yarn you will be using and the stitch size for the project.

CROCHET ABBREVIATIONS

Crochet directions are written in a special shorthand. Once you learn the symbols and abbreviations, it will be much easier to follow the directions than it would be if they were all written out. The following will help you to understand the "language."

beg: beginning
bet: between
ch: chain
cl: cluster
dec: decrease
dc: double crochet
dtr: double triple
hdc: half double crochet
inc: increase
lp: loop
MC: main color
pc: picot
rep: repeat
rnd: round
sc: single crochet
sk: skip
sl st: slip stitch
sp: space
st: stitch
tog: together
tr: treble crochet
yo: yarn over hook
***:** repeat whatever comes after

Asterisk *:* When a group of directions is preceded by an asterisk and followed by a number, this number designates how many times those directions should be repeated. For example, the directions might read: "repeat from * 5 times more." This means that the directions that come after the asterisk should be worked 6 times in all.

Brackets [ ]*:* Often, at the end of a group of directions the number of stitches worked in that row will be included in brackets. This alerts you to how many stitches you should have worked before proceeding to the next row.

Parenthesis ( ): Used to describe pattern stitches, the parenthesis will enclose a series of directions for making the pattern. After the parenthesis there will usually be a direction for the number of times the pattern should be repeated. See the Pineapple Doily, page 41, for examples.

Parentheses are also used in garment projects that include instructions for more than one size garment. Usually the number of stitches for the smallest garment appear first, followed by the numbers for two larger sizes in parenthesis.

Even: When the directions say to work an even row, it means that there are to be no increases or decreases.

ADDING A NEW COLOR

When a pattern calls for more than one color, lay the new yarn strand on top of the row of stitches you are working. Crochet 2 or 3 stitches with the first color. When the new color change is needed, introduce the new color on the last yarn over of the previous stitch. When you're finished with the 2nd color, carry it along for a few stitches; this way it will be secured in the work before you cut it off. Use this procedure when joining a strand of the same color as well.

JOINING CROCHET

If you have several pieces (such as sweater or afghan parts) that must be joined, there are different ways to do it.

One method is the slip stitch. With the hook in top loops of both pieces, make a loose slip stitch and continue across the edges to the end of the row. If you work with right sides facing, the seam ridge will be on the wrong side. If you attach pieces with wrong sides facing, the seams will appear on the right side.

Some patterns call for a single crochet to join pieces. With right sides facing and hook in the top loops at both pieces, work single crochets across the edge to the end of the row.

You can also sew the pieces together with matching yarn and a large-eye yarn needle. With right sides facing, use an overcast stitch through the top loop of each stitch of each piece. Continue across the row.

CROCHET EDGES

Work the first row of single crochet from the right side of the work. Work 1 single crochet in each stitch on the cast-on or bound-off edges. Work 1 single crochet in each knot formed on the side edges. When working around curved edges, it is often necessary to skip stitches in order to get the desired shape.

BLOCKING

It is important to save the labels from your skeins of yarn. Often there is important information about the properties of the yarn and how to care for it. Most acrylic yarns do not need extensive blocking. Usually, a very light steaming with a warm iron is all that is required.

To block wool make a paper pattern of the required size. Pin this to a well-padded ironing board. With the wrong side of your wool piece facing up, pin the edges of the piece to conform to the paper pattern. Cover with a damp cloth and press with a moderately hot iron. Do not use too much pressure, as you will flatten a raised pattern. Leave the piece pinned until it is dry.

MAKING POM-POMS

Some of the projects presented here require a finishing touch of pom-poms, fringes, or tassels. A pom-pom is short and fat; a fringe or tassel (used around a shawl or afghan, for example) might be longer and thinner than the pom-pom. In any case, the instructions for making all of them are the same. The length and amount of yarn to use will vary according to how you want to use it.

1. Cut a piece of cardboard to the size indicated in the directions given with each project.

2. Wind the yarn around the cardboard as many times as indicated in the project directions.

3. Slip the loops off the cardboard. Cut a 12-inch piece of yarn and slip it through the loops. Tie securely.

4. Clip the loops at the untied end, fluff out the pom-pom, and trim evenly to the desired size.

For Your Home

There are many lovely accessories that make a home unique. When you set a table with a handmade place mat, for example, it adds a certain charm to that area of the home. A hand-crocheted afghan done in lacy squares of soft off-white wool makes the sofa or bed on which it rests cozy and inviting.

Stitch a crocheted scallop edge to towels, pillowcases, and other linens, and you've created a look that is at once extra special.

Decorating with handcrafted items is an affordable way to make a statement. It says that the people who live in that home care about their environment. It is inviting to be there. When given as gifts, handmade accessories are always appreciated, for with them you give an extra bit of yourself.

The following projects have been designed to add visual pleasure to your home. They are practical and are a joy to use as well. They will all fit in with any decorating style, which gives them a timeless quality.

Pinwheel Pot Holder

There is no reason to hide your pot holders in a drawer when they are as pretty and colorful as this one. Make a batch in a variety of colors to match your kitchen. They are always best-sellers at bazaars and will certainly be appreciated as gifts.

The yarn used for the pot holder, which is the same yarn used for the place mat on page 31, is cotton, so it is easy to keep clean. Use leftover yarn for this project and it will cost you nothing.

Materials: Bernat Fettuccia cotton yarn—1 ball each in Color A (red) and Color B (white)

Hook: J

DIRECTIONS
This motif uses 2 colors—A and B.

Using Color A, ch 3 and join into ring with a sl st in first ch.

Rnd 1: Ch 1, work 7 sc in ring, join with sl st to first ch.

Rnd 2: Ch 1, join Color B, and work sc in same sp, * sc with Color A and sc with Color B into next st, rep from * to end. Using Color A, join with sl st into first ch.

Rnd 3: Ch 1, working into back half only of each st on every rnd, work 2 sc with Color B into next sc, sc with Color A into next sc. Rep from * to last st, work 2 sc with Color B into last st. Join with a sl st with Color A into first ch.

Rnd 4: Ch 1, * work 2 sc with Color B into next sc, sc with Color B into next sc, sc with Color A into next sc, rep from * to last 2 sts, 2 sc with Color B in next sc, sc with Color B into next sc. Join with sl st with Color A to first ch.

Rnd 5: Ch 1, * work 2 sc with Color B into next sc, sc with Color B into each of next 2 sc, sc with Color A into next sc, rep from * to last 3 sts, 2 sc with Color B into next sc, sc with Color B into each of next 2 sc. Join with sl st with Color A into first ch.

Continue in this way, working 1 more st with Color B in each group on every rnd until there are 8 sts of Color B in each group [63 sts in rnd].

Rnd 10: Ch 1, * work 2 sc with Color A into next sc, sc with Color B into each of next 7 sc, sc with Color A into next sc. Rep from * to end, but do not work last sc with Color A. Join with sl st with Color A into first ch.

Rnd 11: Ch 1, * work 2 sc with Color A into next sc, sc with Color A into each of next 2 sc, sc with Color B into each of next 6 sc, sc with Color A into next sc. Rep from * to end, but do not do last sc with Color A. Join with sl st with Color A into first ch.

Continue in this way, increasing 7 sts in every rnd, but working 1 st less with Color B in each group on every rnd, until 1 st of Color B remains [112 sts in rnd].

Before fastening off, work 1 rnd of sc with Color A.

FINISH

For extra durable pot holder, make 2 and join them together with an edge of sc. End with ch 6, sl st back into first ch to form lp, work 10 sc in lp. Fasten off.

Checkered Pot Holder

Make a country pot holder with an afghan stitch, using red and white cotton yarn, or change the colors to match your kitchen. This design looks good in almost any combination, and, if you expand the directions, you can make place mats to match. The finished size is a generous 7 by 8 inches, and there is a loop for hanging.

Materials: Bernat Fettuccia cotton yarn—1
 skein each in Color A (red) and Color B
 (white)

Hook: H

DIRECTIONS

Using a strand of both colors together, ch 8.

Row 1: Using Color A, insert hook into 2nd ch, yo, draw lp through, (insert hook into next ch, yo, draw lp through) 2 times. Using Color B, (insert hook into next ch, yo, draw lp through) 4 times. Continue in this way, working 4 lps with Color A and 4 lps with Color B.

Row 2: Using Color B, yo, draw through 1 lp, (yo, draw through 2 lps) 3 times. Using Color A, (yo, draw through 2 lps) 4 times. Continue in this way to end.

   Continue in pat and work 4 more rows; then alternate the colors and work 6 rows.

   Rep these 12 rows 3 times.

FINISH

Using 1 strand of each color, sc all around, working 3 sc in each corner, ending with a ch of 10, 1 sc into first ch to make a lp for hanging.

Oval Place Mat

This cotton place mat is made from two strands of white and red yarn plied together to create a tweed effect. You can do this with any combination of colors for an interesting country table covering. This yarn is called "Fettuccia" and looks like thin strands of ribbon. It is fun to work with and the project itself is quick and easy. The finished size is 12 by 15 inches and the materials listed below are enough for four place mats.

Materials: Bernat Fettuccia cotton yarn—5
    skeins each in red and white

Hook: J

DIRECTIONS
Using a strand of each color, ch 8.

Rnd 1: Work 5 dc in 3rd ch from hook, 1 dc in next 4-chs, 6 dc in last lp. Continue around and work 1 dc in other side of the 4 ch lps. Join with sl st at top of the first ch-3.

Rnd 2: Ch 3 [this becomes the first dc], work 1 dc in first st, 2 dc in next 5 sts, 4 dc, 2 dc in next 6 sts. Join rnd in top of ch-3 with sl st.

Rnd 3: Ch 3, work 1 dc in first st, * (1 dc, 2 dc) [inc made] 5 times, 5 dc, (2 dc, 1 dc) 6 times. Join rnd in top of first ch-3 with sl st.

Rnds 4–10: Rep Rnd 3, adding another 1 dc progressively between the 2 dc [incs].

Example: Rnd 4: * (2 dc, 2 dc same st).

        Rnd 6: * (4 dc, 2 dc same st).

        Rnd 10: * (6 dc, 2 dc same st).

Country Place Mat

A lacy, openwork pattern is used to make place mats 12 by 18 inches. (The center band is 4 inches; the side bands, 2.) The soft cotton material is pretty and practical. The earth tone colors give this project a country look, but the yarn comes in a variety of colors from which to choose. You might consider making each place mat in a slightly different color. The materials listed below are enough for four place mats.

Materials: Phildar Akala perle cotton—2 balls each in Color A (dark brown), Color B (rust), Color C (light brown), and Color D (ecru)

Hook: F

DIRECTIONS
Make a foundation ch of 50 sts with Color A.

Pattern
Row 1: Hdc in 2nd ch from hook, hdc in next ch, * ch 2, sk 2 chs, hdc in next 2 chs, rep from * across, end ch 1, turn.

Row 2: Hdc in first 2 hdc, * ch 2, 2 hdc in next 2 hdc, ch 1, turn. Rep Row 2 for st pat.

Work 7 rows of pat in Color A, 7 rows of pat in Color B, 7 rows of pat in Color C, 14 rows of pat in Color D, 7 rows of pat in Color C, 7 rows of pat in Color B, and 7 rows of pat in Color A.

FINISH
Block the finished place mat by placing it, face down, on your ironing board and pressing with a medium-hot steam iron. To make sure it is perfectly even on each side, you might pin each corner to the padded ironing board. Measure each side and adjust it to be the same on each corresponding side. Press again.

Lacy Wool Afghan

This afghan is made with an ecru or off-white wool yarn. Each granny square is a lacy pattern that, when assembled, creates a lovely overall design. The blanket is light and airy looking, but warm and luxurious feeling.

While this afghan is made to fit a single-size bed, if you add squares, you can adjust it to fit any size bed or sofa. The finished measurement is 5 by 7 feet.

Materials: Phildar Suffrage #249 wool (50-gr. balls)—24 balls in ecru color
Large-eye darning needle

Hook: H

Gauge: Each square = 6 inches

DIRECTIONS

Granny Square Pattern: (Make 154)
Ch 6. Join with sl st to form ring.

Rnd 1: Ch 3, (yo, insert hook in ring and draw up lp, yo and draw through 2 lps on hook) 2 times; yo and draw through all 3 lps on hook [first cl made], * ch 5, (yo, insert hook in ring and draw up lp, yo and draw through 2 lps on hook) 3 times; yo and draw through all 4 lps on hook [another cl made], ch 1, work cl. Rep from * 2 times more, ch 5, work cl, ch 1, join with sl st in top of first cl.

Rnd 2: Sl st in next ch-5 sp, work first cl in same sp, ch 3, work another cl in same sp [first corner made], * ch 1, work 3 dc in next ch-1 sp, ch 1, in next ch-5 sp work cl, ch 3, and cl [another corner made]. Rep from * 2 times more, ch 1, work 3 dc in next sp, ch 1, join to first cl.

Rnd 3: Sl st in next ch-3 sp, work first corner in same sp, * ch 2, dc in next sp, dc in each of next 3 dc, dc in next sp, ch 2, work corner in next sp. Rep from * 2 times more, ch 2, dc in next sp, dc in each of next 3 dc, dc in next sp, ch 2, join.

Rnd 4: Sl st in next ch-3 sp, work first corner in same sp, * ch 2, dc in next sp and in each dc to next sp, dc in sp, ch 2, work corner in next sp. Rep from * 2 times more, ch 2, dc in next sp, dc in each dc to next sp, dc in sp, ch 2, join.

Rnd 5: Rep Rnd 4. Fasten off.

FINISH

Arrange rows of 11 squares across and 14 down. Join tog from the wrong side with a sc through each pair of corresponding dc, picking up back lps of dc only and working 1 sc in corner sps.

After all squares are joined, attach yarn to a square after a 3-dc cl in the ch-2 sp.

Rnd 1: Ch 3 [first dc], 1 dc in each dc of square [9 dc]. Work 1 dc in ch-2 sp, ch 2, 1 cl as in squares in corner, ch 2, 1 cl in corner, ch 2.

Continue in this way all around afghan. Join with a sl st in ch-3 [first dc]. When you come to each of 4 corners, work 2 cls separated by a ch-3.

Rnd 2: Ch 3 [first dc], work 1 dc in each of the next 10 dc, * 1 dc in ch-2 sp, ch 2 [1 cl of 5 joined], dc in ch-2 sp, ch 2, 1 dc in ch-2 sp, 11 dc. *

Rep around bet *'s, ending with sl st into 3rd ch of first dc. Fasten off.

Basket of Roses Picture

You can crochet this lovely basket of flowers to create a framed picture. It's a nice way to extend your craft for a decorative touch in any room. The basket is a lacy crochet pattern with scalloped edges, and the flower stems are simple chains. Each flower is made with a different color of perle cotton, which is available in a profusion of gorgeous colors. Make a bouquet to fit your room colors.

The pattern for the flowers can also be used to make appliqués for hats and mittens or to decorate a sweater. Each is approximately 2 inches across.

Materials for Picture: Phildar Akala or Coats & Clark perle cotton #5 or #8—small amounts in fuchsia, coral, royal blue, ecru, green, and baby blue

Frame

Glue

Mat Board

Materials for Framing and Mounting Picture

1 piece pink calico cotton fabric, 14 by 18 inches

1 piece solid lavender cotton fabric, 14 by 18 inches

1 piece fusible webbing, 14 by 18 inches

2 pieces white cardboard, 14 by 18 inches

Prefabricated picture frame, 12 by 16 inches

Craft knife

White glue

Straightedge

Hooks: Steel #00 and #2

DIRECTIONS FOR PICTURE

Roses: (Use #00 hook)

Wind yarn 3 or 4 times around your finger. Remove lps from your finger and fasten with sl st.

Rnd 1: Ch 1, work 17 sc into ring, sl st to first ch.

Rnd 2: Ch 6, sk 2 sc, 1 hdc into next sc, * ch 4, sk 2 sc, 1 hdc into next sc. Rep from * 3 times more, ch 4, sl st into 2nd of first ch-4.

Rnd 3: Work (1 sc, 1 hdc, 3 dc, 1 hdc, 1 sc) into each 4-ch lp, end with sl st into first sc.

Rnd 4: Sl st into back of hdc on Rnd 2, * ch 5, keeping yarn at back of work, sl st into back of next hdc on Rnd 2. Rep from * 4 times more, ch 5, sl st into same hdc as first sl st.

Rnd 5: Work (1 sc, 1 hdc, 5 dc, 1 hdc, 1 sc) into each ch-5 lp, end with sl st to first sc.

Rnd 6: Sl st into back of sl st on Rnd 4, * ch 6, keeping yarn at back of work, sl st into next sl st on Rnd 4. Rep from * to end.

Rnd 7: Work (1 sc, 1 hdc, 7 dc, 1 hdc, 1 sc) into each ch-6 lp, end with sl st into first sc. Fasten off.

Stems

Using green yarn and #2 hook, make ch of multiples of 5 plus 1 (i.e.: 11, 16, 21). Sc in 2nd ch from hook and sc in each ch. Fasten off.

Leaves

Using #2 hook, ch 12, work 1 sc in 2nd ch from hook, * 1 hdc in next 2 ch, 1 dc in next 2 ch, 1 tr in next ch, 1 dc in next 2 ch, 1 hdc in next 2 ch, * 3 sc in last ch.

Turn work and work sts starting from * to * on other side of ch, ending with sl st into first sc. Fasten off.

Basket

Using #2 hook and ecru color, make foundation ch of 23.

Rnd 1: Work 1 dc in 3rd ch from hook, 1 dc in all ch sts. Ch 3, turn work.

40

Rnd 2: Work 1 dc in first ch, and 1 dc in all sts across until last dc. Work 2 dc in last st. Ch 3, turn [22 dc].

Rnd 3: Work 1 dc in first ch, sk 1 st, work 2 dc in next st across row. Ch 3, turn work.

Rnds 4–7: Rep Rnd 3 4 more times.

Rnd 8: Rep Rnd 3, with 1 ch between each pair of dc.

Rnds 9–12: Rep Rnd 8.

Rnd 13: Work 5 dc in first ch, * sc in ch-1 sp, 10 dc in next ch-1 sp *. Rep across row bet *'s, ending with 6 dc in last dc. Fasten off.

Directions For Framing and Mounting Picture

1. Cut fusible webbing same size as each piece of fabric and fuse to each piece of fabric and cardboard with a hot iron. Cut both pieces to fit frame.

2. Measure 1 inch in from all sides and draw a border line on the calico fabric. To make the angled corners, measure 4 inches in from each corner both horizontally and vertically. Mark these points on border line. Join all the marks with lines. Using a sharp craft knife, cut the inside shape away from the calico border, leaving a mat border.

3. Place the mat border on top of lavender fabric board and place both over backing cardboard of frame. Place sandwich of boards in frame without glass and secure according to frame directions.

4. Assemble all the crochet elements. Position basket and flowers with stems and leaves in place on lavender fabric background. Take the time to move them around until you have the arrangement of colors and shapes that pleases you.

5. Put a drop of white glue at various points on the back of each element and place back in position on fabric background. Set it aside to dry for a few minutes. When gluing the stems, glue one end, let it dry, then glue other end and then middle. If you use a toothpick, it will be easy to apply a small drop of glue.

6. When all is dry, fluff up each flower so it stands out.

Pineapple Doily

The pineapple design is probably the most popular of crochet patterns. It has been recreated in hundreds of ways for doilies, place mats, bedspreads, and afghans.

The table doily is approximately 16 inches across and is made with cotton Speed Cro-Sheen. It is not too delicate to use as a place mat and is completely washable.

Materials: Coats & Clark Speed Cro-Sheen—
   1 ball, white

Hook: C

DIRECTIONS
Starting at center, ch 12. Join with sl st to form ring.

Rnd 1: Ch 3, work 31 dc in ring. Join to 3rd ch of ch-3.

Rnd 2: Ch 8, * sk 3 dc, dc in next dc, ch 5. Rep from * around. Join to 3rd ch of ch-8.

Rnd 3: Ch 3, * work 6 dc in next sp, dc in next dc. Rep from * around. Join.

Rnd 4: Ch 5, holding back on hook the last lp of each dtr, make 2 dtr in same place as sl st, yo and draw through all lps on hook [cl made]; ch 12, sc in 6th ch from hook [picot made], ch 6, sk 6 dc, make a 3-dtr cl in next dc. Rep from * around. Join to tip of first cl.

Rnd 5: Sl st in next 6 chs and in picot, ch 4, work 9 tr in same picot, * ch 8, 10 tr in next picot. Rep from * around. Join.

Rnd 6: Ch 5, (tr in next tr, ch 1) 8 times; tr in next tr, * ch 4, tr in next sp, ch 4, (tr in next tr, ch 1) 9 times. Rep from * around. Join.

Rnd 7: Sl st in next sp, sc in same sp, * (ch 3, sc in next sp) 8

times; ch 4, sk next sp, 2 dc in next tr, ch 4, sk next sp, sc in next sp. Rep from * around. Join.

Rnd 8: Sl st in next lp, sc in same lp, * (ch 3, sc in next lp) 7 times; ch 4, dc in next 2 dc, ch 4, sk next sp, sc in next lp. Rep from * around. Join.

Rnd 9: Sl st in next lp, sc in same lp, * (ch 3, sc in next lp) 6 times; ch 4, dc in next dc, ch 1, dc in next dc, ch 4, sk next sp, sc in next lp. Rep from * around. Join.

Rnd 10: Sl st in next lp, sc in same lp, * (ch 3, sc in next lp) 5 times; ch 4, dc in next dc, dc in ch-1 sp, dc in next dc, ch 4, sk next sp, sc in next lp. Rep from * around. Join.

Rnd 11: Sl st in next lp, sc in same lp, * (ch 3, sc in next lp) 4 times; ch 4, work 2 dc in each of next 3 dc, ch 4, sk next sp, sc in next lp. Rep from * around. Join.

Rnd 12: Sl st in next lp, sc in same lp, * (ch 3, sc in next lp) 3 times; ch 4, 2 dc in each of next 6 dc, ch 4, sk next sp, sc in next lp. Rep from * around. Join.

Rnd 13: Sl st in next lp, sc in same lp, * (ch 3, sc in next lp) 2 times; ch 4, dc in next dc, work 2 dc in each of next 10 dc, dc in next dc, ch 4, sk next sp, sc in next lp. Rep from * around. Join.

Rnd 14: Sl st in next lp, sc in same lp, * ch 3, sc in next lp, ch 4, dc in each dc across, ch 4, sk next sp, sc in next lp. Rep from * around. Join.

Rnd 15: Sl st to center of lp, sc in same lp, * ch 5, dc in each dc across, ch 5, sk next sp, sc in next lp. Rep from * around. Join. Fasten off.

Log Cabin Afghan

The Log Cabin design has always been one of the most popular in quiltmaking. In recent years this design has been translated to knit and crochet projects, and I've included a different version of it in my last two books. Once again, it's offered here in a completely new color scheme that I think you'll enjoy.

This is an easy project to crochet; the individual squares are large and can be stitched together quickly. The finished project is 56 by 56 inches and is made up of sixteen squares, each 14 by 14 inches. If you want to make it longer, add eight more squares.

Materials: Unger Aries knitting worsted weight yarn (3½-oz. skeins)—5 skeins in Color A (wine), 3 skeins in Color B (white), 9 skeins in Color C (navy blue), 5 skeins in Color D (light blue), 8 skeins in Color E (royal blue), and 7 skeins in Color F (gray)

Hook: H

Gauge: Each square = 14 inches

DIRECTIONS
Refer to Diagram for Color Chart sequence.

Center
With Color A, ch 15.

Row 1: Work 1 sc in 3rd ch from hook; (ch 1, sk 1, ch 1, sc in next ch) 6 times.

Row 2: Ch 2, turn. Work 1 sc in first ch-1 sp, (ch 1, 1 sc in next ch-1 sp) 5 times; ch 1, 1 sc in sp under ch-2 at end of row.

Rows 3–14: Rep Row 2 12 times. At end of Row 14, change to Color B in last sc.

To change colors: Work last sc in row until there are 2 lps on hook. Leave 4-inch ends and finish off color being used. With new color, yo and draw through 2 lps on hook. You now have a color change.

Color B Band
Row 1: Ch 2, turn; working back across row just worked, work 1 sc in first ch-1 sp, (ch 1, 1 sc in next ch-1 sp) 5 times; ch 1, work (1 sc, ch 2, 1 sc) in ch-2 sp at end of row for corner.

Continuing across side edge of A center, (ch 1, sk next row, 1 sc in next row) 6 times; ch 1, sk last row, 1 sc in beg ch of foundation ch.

Row 2: Ch 2, turn; work (1 sc, ch 1) in each ch-1 sp to ch-2 sp at corner; work (1 sc, ch 2, 1 sc) in corner sp, work (ch 1, 1 sc) in each ch-1 sp across, ending ch 1, 1 sc in sp under turning ch.

Rows 3–7: Rep Row 2 5 times. At end of Row 7, change to Color C in last sc.

Color C Band
Row 1: Ch 1, do not turn. Working across ends of B rows and along beg row of A center, work (1 sc in next row, ch 1, sk next row) 3 times; 1 sc in first sc of A center; (ch 1, 1 sc in next ch-1 sp) 6 times. Ch 1, work (1 sc, ch 2, 1 sc) in ch-2 sp at corner. Working across side edge of A center and ends of B band, (ch 1, 1 sc in next row, sk next row) 6 times; (ch 1, 1 sc in next row) 2 times [1 row of each color]; (ch 1, sk next row, 1 sc in next row) 3 times.

Rows 2–7: Rep Rows 2–7 of B band. At end of Row 7, change to D band in last sc.

Color D Band
On first row, work across ends of C band.

Row 1: Ch 2, do not turn; work (1 sc in next row, ch 1, sk next row) 3 times; ch 1, 1 sc in turning-ch sp at beg of next color band. Work (ch 1, 1 sc in next ch-1 sp) in each ch-1 sp to corner; ch 1, work (1 sc, ch 2, 1 sc) in corner sp; work (ch 1, 1 sc in next ch-1

sp) in each ch-1 sp to beg of next color band; ch 1, 1 sc in first row [at end of next color band]; (ch 1, sk next row, 1 sc in next row) 3 times.

Rows 2–7: Rep Rows 2–7 of B band. At end of Row 7, change to E in last sc.

Color E Band
On first row, work across ends of D band and along last row of C band. Work same as D band. At end of last row, change to Color B in last sc.

Color B Band
On first row, work across ends of E band and along last row of D band. At end of last row, change to Color F in last sc.

Color F Band
On first row, work across ends of B band and along last row of E band. Work same as D band. At end of last row, finish off.

Make 16 blocks.

Joining Blocks
Follow Diagram and arrange squares as shown. To join, hold 2 squares with right sides together, and sew or sc blocks tog with 4 squares across and 4 squares down. Join the squares in rows and then join the rows.

Edging
With right sides facing, join C with sl st in any outer corner sp of afghan.

Row 1: Ch 1, work (1 sc, ch 2, 1 sc, ch 1) in same sp; work (1 sc, ch 1) in each ch sp of squares' outside borders, and, in each remaining corner sp, work (1 sc, ch 2, 1 sc, ch 1). Join with sl st in beg sc.

Row 2: Ch 1, turn; sl st into ch-1 sp, ch 1; 1 sc in same sp, ch 1. Work (1 sc, ch 1) in each ch-1 sp around. In each corner sp, work (1 sc, ch 2, 1 sc, ch 1). Join with sl st in beg sc.

Rep row 2 times more. Turn and join with sl st in any corner sp.

Row 5: Ch 1, work (1 sc, ch 2, 1 sc, ch 1) in same sp. Complete row in same manner as Row 2.

Rows 6–8: Rep Row 2 3 times. At end of Row 8, finish off.

FINISH
Weave in all ends, and, if necessary, block around border.

Log Cabin Afghan

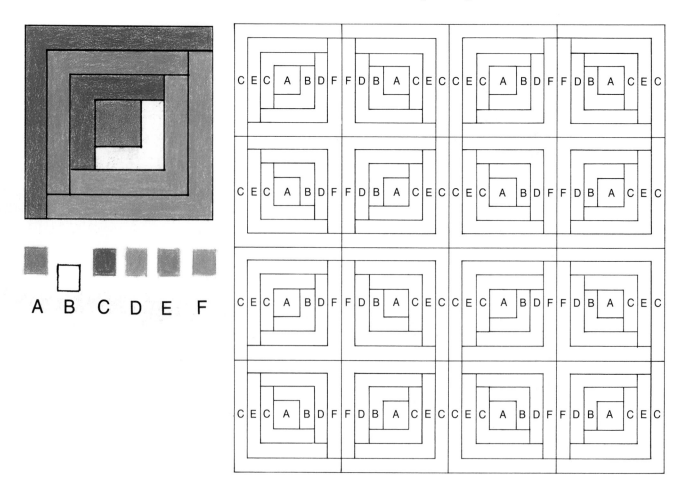

Lacy Towel Edgings

Our grandmothers and great grandmothers had the time and patience to create some of the finest lacy crochet edgings for towels, runners, aprons, and pillowcases. We still appreciate this kind of wonderful handwork, but few of us have the time to work with such fine thread on a hook that is not much larger than a needle.

Since this work is still so valued for its beauty, I wanted to include a few edgings in the book. To simplify some of the old designs, I used crochet cotton and a larger hook. Both of the edgings here are for scalloped motifs and are quite lovely when worked in white and added to white hand towels.

Materials: Coats & Clark Speed Cro-Sheen,
    or perle cotton #20—1 ball in white

Hook: #9

DIRECTIONS

Edging A

This edging is approximately 1½ inches deep. Beg with a ch slightly longer than desired length.

Row 1: Sc in 2nd ch from hook and in next 3 ch, * ch 5, sk next 4 ch, dc in next 5 ch, ch 5, sk next 4 ch, sc in next 7 ch. Rep from * across for length desired. End with 4 sc instead of 7 sc. Cut off remaining ch. Ch 1, turn.

Row 2: Sc in first 3 sc, * ch 5, sk next 4 ch, dc in next ch, dc in next 2 dc, ch 3, sk next dc, dc in next 2 dc, dc in next ch, ch 5, sk next sc, sc in next 5 sc. Rep from * across, ending with sc in last 3 sc. Ch 1, turn.

Row 3: Sc in first 2 sc, * ch 5, sk next 3 ch, dc in next 2 ch, dc in next dc, ch 5, sc in next ch-3 sp, ch 5, sk next 2 dc, dc in next dc, dc in next 2 ch, ch 5, sk next sc, sc in next 3 sc. Rep from * across, ending with sc in last 2 sc. Ch 1, turn.

Row 4: Sc in first sc, * ch 5, sk next 3 ch, dc in next 2 ch, dc in next dc, ch 5, sc in next ch-5 lp, ch 7, sc in next ch-5 lp, ch 5, sk next 2 dc, dc in next dc, dc in next 2 ch, ch 5, sk next sc, sc in next sc. Rep from * across. Turn.

Row 5: Sl st in first 4 ch, ch 3, dc in next ch, dc in next dc, * ch 5, sk next ch-5 lp. Holding back on hook the last lp of each tr, make 3 tr in the next ch-7 lp, yo and draw through all lps on hook [cl made]; work (ch 5, sc in 5th ch from hook, make cl in same ch-7 lp) 4 times; ch 5, sk next 2 dc, dc in next dc, dc in next 2 ch; sk next sc and next 3 ch; dc in next 2 ch, dc in next dc. Rep from * across. End with dc in the last dc and following 2 ch. Fasten off.

Edging B
This edging is approximately 1 inch deep. Beg with a ch longer than desired length.

Row 1: Sc in 2nd ch from hook and in each ch across, having a number of sc divisible by 16 plus 8. Cut off extra ch. Ch 4, turn.

Row 2: Holding back on hook last lp for each tr, make tr in next 3 sc, yo and draw through all lps on hook [starting cl made]; * ch 3; holding back on hook last lp of each tr, tr in next 4 sc, yo and draw through all lps on hook [cl made]. Rep from * across. Ch 1, turn.

Row 3: Sl st in the next sp, ch 1, sc in same sp, * ch 1, sk next sp; in next sp make (dtr, ch 1) 8 times and dtr; ch 1, sk next sp, sc in next sp. Rep from * across, sl st to tip of last cl. Ch 5, turn.

Row 4: Sk next dtr, sc in next sp, * (ch 3, sc in next sp) 7 times; ch 2, sk next dtr, next sc, and following dtr; sc in next sp. Rep from * across, end last rep with ch 5 instead of ch 2, sl st in tip of last cl. Fasten off.

FINISH
Place edgings on padded ironing board and steam-press so they lie flat. Position trim on towel or pillowcase and st along sides and top edge. Tack here and there to hold in place.

Commuter Afghan

The ripple, or chevron, is a most popular pattern for afghans. This one, designed by Anne Lane, can be easily carried to and from work, as the finished project is made up of strips that are later sewed together. Each strip of color is 5 by 6 inches. This is a good lap project that can be made in any color combination and size. This one is made in lovely earth tones of rust, dark brown, and off-white for contrast. The finished size is 55 by 61 inches.

Materials: Knitting worsted weight yarn
   (3¾-oz. skeins)—3 skeins in Color A
   (white), 4 skeins in Color B (brown), and
   4 skeins in Color C (rust)

Hook: I

DIRECTIONS
You will be making 3 strips of Color A and 4 strips each of Colors B and C.

Row 1: Ch 22, sc in 2nd ch from hook and in each of next 9 ch, 3 sc in next ch, sc in next 10 ch, ch 1, and turn.

Row 2: Working in *back lps* only, sc in first sc, sk next sc, sc in 9 sc, 3 sc in next sc, sc in 9 sc, sk 1 sc, sc in last sc, ch 1, and turn.
   Rep Row 2 until the piece measures 6 inches or desired length.

FINISH
Sl st strips tog in following color order: B, C, A, B, C, A, C, B, A, C, and B.

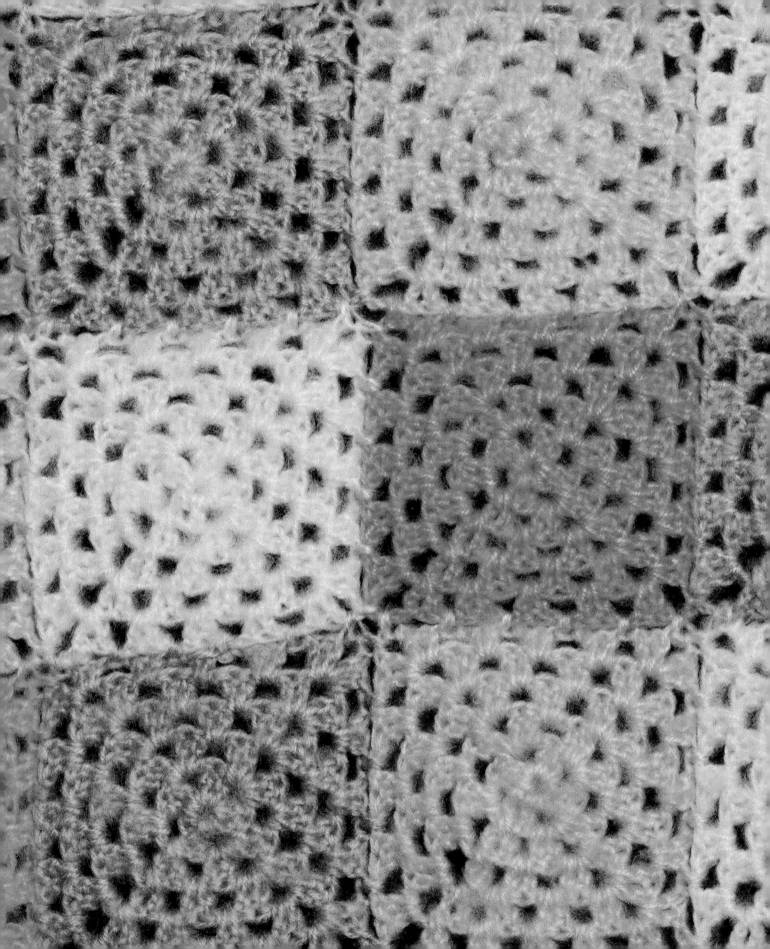

Personally Yours

Most of us craft for gift giving and, while every one of these projects makes a wonderful gift, you will find it hard to part with them.

The Kenya-style bag, for example, is made with cotton Creole, a cotton twist that is soft, yet durable. The pastel colors make up the striped pattern that will complement any spring wardrobe. This is a quick and easy project, as are most of them.

Imagine whipping up in one evening a soft, fluffy mohair cap to match a coat or jacket! For traveling, the granny slippers are a snap to make. Tuck them in your overnight bag and you're all set.

When did you last have time to make something just for you? Now is the time to try a one-size-fits-all sweater, or the wonderful French blue and white one with checks and stripes. It looks good on any shape!

My favorite is the little evening bag just big enough for the tiniest essentials. The yarn we used is a brand new silky ribbon in the most smashing, nighttime colors. It almost looks beaded.

Three-Color Sweater Jacket and Hat

Crochet a sweater jacket in a smart three-color combination to go with any outfit. Here I've used a blending of similar shades of pink for a lacy-look granny square project. It's easy to carry along while working on it, and it makes a nice lap project when you are stitching the squares together.

Add interesting buttons, a zipper, or crocheted ties to the front opening. This is a pretty and practical garment to own or to give as a gift. It's made with an acrylic/wool blend of knitting worsted.

Materials: Phildar Pegase knitting worsted weight yarn (1¾-oz. skeins)—8 skeins in Color A (pink), 8 skeins in Color B (old rose), and 3 skeins in Color C (wine)
Yarn needle
5 buttons

Hook and Gauge: G hook = 4-inch square
H hook = 4¼-inch square
I hook = 4½-inch square

DIRECTIONS

Body
With size G (H) (I) hook and using Color C, ch 6, join with sl st in first ch to form ring.

Rnd 1: Ch 3, 2 dc in ring * ch 1, 3 dc in ring; rep from * 2 times. Ch 1, join with sl st in top of ch-3 [ch-3 counts as 1 dc]. Fasten off.

Rnd 2: Join next Color A in any ch-1 sp. Ch 3 in same sp. Work 2 dc, ch 1, 3 dc for first corner. * Ch 1 in next ch-1 sp. Work 3 dc. Ch 1, 3 dc [corner]. Rep from * 2 times. Ch 1. Join.

Rnd 3: Continue with Color A. Ch 4. Work a corner in corner sp. * Work 3 dc, ch 1, 3 dc. Ch 1, 3 dc in next ch-1 sp. Ch 1, rep from * 3 times until last dc. Work 2 dc. Join with sl st in ch-3. Fasten off.

Rnd 4: Join Color B in any corner sp, ch 3 in same sp, 2 dc, ch 1, 3 dc, work (ch 1, 3 dc in next ch-1 sp) 2 times. Ch 1, make a corner in next corner sp, rep from * 2 times, work (ch 1, 3 dc in next ch-1 sp) 2 times, ch 1. Join; fasten off.

When working 2 or more rows in same color, sl st to corner before working rnd.

Make 81 granny squares.

Sew squares tog from right side, using an overcast st and working through back lps only. Sew st for st.

Follow body pattern for sewing squares tog. Fold sides over back (right sides tog) and sew shoulders tog between arrows.

Sew sleeves tog, as shown in Diagram, using 15 squares, and make a tube by sewing points A tog and sewing across to points B. Set sleeves into arm openings.

Cuff

Attach Color B at sleeve edge with sl st.

Rnd 1: Ch 1, * insert hook in next st, yo, pull lp through. Rep once more to make a dec of 1 st. Rep from * around cuff edge. Join with sl st to ch-1.

Rnd 2: Ch 1, * dec 1 st, 1 sc. * Rep bet *'s around. Join with sl st in ch-1 sp.

Rnd 3: Ch 1, 1 sc in each st around. Join with sl st in ch-1 sp. Rep Rnd 3 20 times or desired length to make cuff. Fasten off.

FINISH

Attach yarn at 1 bottom corner of front opening. Work 1 row of sc around edge. Make lps for buttons at desired places by chaining 10 sts and sl st in first ch. Continue working sc between lps. Join at bottom edge and fasten off.

Weave ends back into wrong side with a darning needle. Sew on buttons.

Hat

Sew 5 squares tog, as shown in Diagram.

Sew all corner edges tog and continue seam to top of corner 0.

Attach Color B to bottom edge. Ch 3 and work dc around entire edge. Join with sl st in top of ch-3. Rep this dc row 10 times to form brim. Fasten off. Fold brim back for an extra-warm hat.

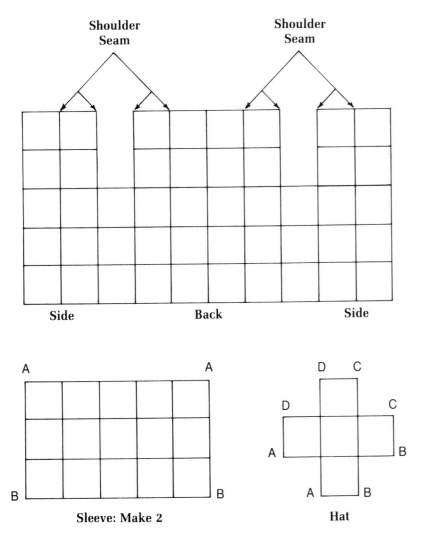

Sleeve: Make 2

Hat

Mohair Shawl

Make a soft and fluffy summer shawl of pastel mohair squares. The finished size is small enough to make this an easy-to-carry-along project. In fact, you can make it as one piece, attaching each new color as you go, or make individual squares to be joined later.

One of my craft workers found this project to be troublesome; another found it quite easy. If you have a problem on the 5th round that connects the squares, you might prefer making the individual squares for later attachment.

Only 2 skeins of each color are needed, making this a very inexpensive project. The tassels do use up more yarn, but, if you don't want to buy more yarn for the multicolored fringe, there will be enough left over of the one color for the fringe.

Materials: Unger Fluffy (50-gr. skeins)—2 skeins each in Color A (blue), Color B (white), Color C (pink), and Color D (green)

Hook: F

Gauge: Each square = 3½ inches

DIRECTIONS
Work from 1 to 63, following Chart and using colors as noted.

Triangle 1
With Color A, ch 5.

Row 1: Work 2 dc, ch 2, 2 dc, ch 1, dc in 5th ch from hook. Ch 4, turn.

Row 2: Work 2 dc in next ch-1 sp, ch 1, make a corner (corner =

2 dc, ch 2, 2 dc) in next ch-2 sp, ch 1, 2 dc in top of turning ch, ch 1, dc in next ch of turning ch. Ch 4, turn.

Row 3: Work (2 dc in next ch-1 sp, ch 1) 2 times, make a corner (corner = 2 dc, ch 2, 2 dc) in next ch-2 sp, ch 1, 2 dc in next ch-1 sp, ch 1, 2 dc in top of turning ch, ch 1, dc in 3rd ch of turning ch. Ch 4, turn.

Row 4: Rep Row 3, having 1 more group of 2 dc before and after corner.

Row 5: Rep Row 4. End off.

Square 2

With Color B, ch 4, join with sl st to form ring.

Rnd 1: Ch 3 [counts as 1 dc], dc in ring, ch 2, * work 2 dc in ring, ch 2, rep from * 2 times, join last ch-2 to top of ch-3 with a sl st [4 groups of 2 dc in ring].

Rnd 2: Ch 3, dc in last ch-2 sp of Rnd 1 [half-corner], ch 1, * work 2 dc, ch 2, 2 dc in next ch-2 sp [corner], ch 1, rep from * 2 times, make a half-corner of 2 dc in last sp, ch 2, sl st in top of starting ch [8 groups of 2 dc—4 corners].

Rnd 3: Ch 3, dc in last ch-2 sp of previous rnd [half-corner], ch 1, * work 2 dc in next ch-1 sp, ch 1, make a corner of 2 dc, ch 2, 2 dc in next sp, ch 1, rep from * 2 times, work 2 dc in next ch-1 sp, ch 1, make a half-corner of 2 dc in last sp, ch 2, sl st in top of starting ch-3.

Rnd 4: Rep Rnd 3, having 1 more 2 dc bet corners.

Rnd 5: Ch 3, dc in last ch-2 sp of previous rnd [half-corner], ch 1, work (2 dc in next ch-1 sp, ch 1) 3 times.

Joining

Work 2 dc in corner ch-2 sp, ch 1. With wrong sides facing, sc in ch-2 sp of corner of triangle, ch 1, 2 dc in same corner ch-2 sp on square, sc in next ch-1 sp on triangle, work (2 dc in next ch-1 sp on square, sc in next ch-1 sp on triangle) 3 times, 2 dc in corner ch-2 sp of square, sc in next sp of triangle, ch 1, 2 dc in same corner ch-2 sp of square. Complete rnd as for Rnd 4, having 1 more group of 2 dc bet corners. End off. Join 1 side of squares 3, 4, 5, 6, 7, 8, 9, 10, 11, 12, 13, 14 in sequence, as shown on Chart in same manner as square 2 was joined to triangle 1. Work triangle 15 to corner on Row 5. Join to 1 side of square 14 to correspond to opposite side.

Mohair Shawl

1A	2B	3C	4D	5A	6B	7C	8D	9A	10B	11C	12D	13A	14B	15C
16D	17A	18B	19C	20D	21A	22B	23C	24D	25A	26B	27C	28D		
29C	30D	31A	32B	33C	34D	35A	36B	37C	38D	39A				
40B	41C	42D	43A	44B	45C	46D	47A	48B						
49A	50B	51C	52D	53A	54B	55C								
56D	57A	58B	59C	60D										
61C	62D	63A												

Triangle 16

With D, work Rows 1–4 same as for triangle 1.

Row 5: Work to corner; work 2 dc, ch 1 in corner ch-2 sp. With wrong sides facing, sc in corner ch-2 sp of square 2, ch 1, 2 dc in same ch-2 sp on triangle. Continue to join same as other squares. End off.

Square 17

With A, work Rnds 1–4 same as for square 2.

Rnd 5: Work to corner; work 2 dc, ch 1 in corner ch-2 sp. With wrong sides facing, sc in corner ch-2 sp of square 3, ch 1, 2 dc in same ch-2 sp on square 17. Continue to join to 1 side of square 3 and 1 side of triangle 16. Finish rnd, end off.

Square 18
With B, work Rnds 1–4 same as for square 2.

Rnd 5: Work to corner. Work 2 dc, ch 1 in corner, ch-2 sp. Join to 1 side of square 4 and 1 side of square 17. Continue in this way, following Chart for placement and color sequence of squares and triangles.

FINISH
Run in yarn ends on wrong side. With Color A, work 1 row sc across long end of shawl.

Fringe
Cut A, B, C, and D into 20-inch lengths. Using 4 strands tog, fold in half, pull lp through sp, pull 8 ends through lp; tighten knot. Knot a fringe in each sp on sides and bottom of shawl, using same color yarn as triangles.

Scalloped Evening Bag

There is always a time when a small bag comes in handy. Meant to carry "mad money" or cosmetics, this lacy, scallop-edged purse measures 5 inches square when closed. The self-fastening flap is made from a chain of single crochets. You might consider making it with 2 loops on the back for attaching to a belt, rather than making it as an over-the-shoulder item.

The yarn used here is an exciting-looking shimmer of variegated viscose from Phildar. It comes in many of the newest mixed and solid colors. This one is called "Hong Kong," and combines red, purple, brown, and greenish blue. I think it is one of the prettiest of these yarns and could be used to make a beautiful camisole top, as well.

The spools of yarn are small, only 25 grams each, but they go a long way and not much is needed.

Materials: Phildar Look Phil 394 (25-gr. spools)—2 spools in Hong Kong color

Hook: D

Gauge:
6 sts = 1 inch
8 rows = 1 inch

DIRECTIONS

Body of Purse
Make a foundation ch of 30. Starting with 2nd st from hook * work in sc across row. Ch 1, turn *. Rep bet *'s, until entire piece is 11 inches long.

Flap Pattern

Row 1: Work 1 sc in 2nd st from hook, * sk 3 sp, work 7 dc, sk 3 sts, 1 sc into next st. Rep from * to end. Ch 3, turn.

Row 2: Work 1 dc into sc, * ch 3, sc in 4th of 7 dc, ch 3, 2 dc in sc. Rep from * to the end. Ch 1, turn.

Row 3: * Work 1 sc bet 2 dc, 7 dc in sc, rep from * to end. Sc between dc and turning ch. Ch 4, turn.

  Rep Rows 2 and 3.

FINISH

Fold purse in half, bringing bottom edge up, so that purse front measures about 4½ inches. There will be about 4 rows plus flap extended above purse opening. (See Diagram.)

  Sc sides tog. Make a ch of 100 sc, or desired length, for strap and attach it at each side where front and back join.

Mostly Mohair Cap

This warm, fluffy cap is easy to make in one evening. The yarn is a blend of mostly mohair with a small amount of wool and nylon. It's new from Phildar and comes in seven different color combinations that include the exciting colors of electric blue, neon red, fuchsia, and more. Each is plied with gray or black, so it appears as though you've used various yarns together.

The cap is made to fit any size, and the rim can be rolled, turned up as a fat, wide cuff, or rolled twice to create a thick band. Anyway you wear it, this cap looks great.

When finished, brush the yarn a bit to fluff it out.

Materials: Phildar Ladina (approximately 3-oz. skeins)—2 skeins in blue/gray (color Encre #34)

Hook: K

DIRECTIONS
Beg ring with ch 4. Join with sl st.

Rnd 1: Work 8 sc in ring. Join with sl st to first sc.

Rnd 2: Ch 3 [counts as 1 dc], dc same sc as joining, 2 dc in each sc around. Join with sl st to top of ch-3 [16 dc, counting ch-3 as 1 dc].

Rnd 3: Ch 3, 2 dc in next dc [inc made], * dc in next dc, 2 dc in next dc, rep from * around. Join to top of ch-3 [24 dc]. [Always count ch-3 as 1 dc.]

Rnd 4: Ch 3, dc in next dc, 2 dc in next dc, * dc in each of next 2 dc, 2 dc in next dc. Rep from * around. Join [8 incs made].

Rnd 5: Ch 3, dc in each dc around, increasing 8 dc evenly spaced around [having 1 more dc bet incs than on previous inc rnd—40 dc].

Rnd 6: Rep Rnd 5, ending with 48 dc.

Rnd 7: Ch 3, dc in each dc around. Join.

Rnd 8: Rep Rnd 7 10 times or enough to achieve desired length. Break off and fasten.

Circular Bag

Make a circular bag with black, gray, and red cotton yarn for a dramatic bull's-eye design.

The finished size is 12 inches across with a circumference of approximately 37 inches. The front and back pieces are joined with a 2-inch-wide strap that continues for over-the-shoulder length. A decorative button is attached to the front of one top edge with a corresponding loop on the other for easy closure.

Materials: Bernat Fettuccia 100% cotton
string—1 ball in Color A (scarlet #8333),
1 ball in Color B (pearl gray #8392), and
3 balls in Color C (black #8394)

Hook: H

DIRECTIONS

Bag Circle: (Make 2).
Using Color A, ch 4, join to form lp.

Rnd 1: Work 10 sc in lp, join with sl st.

Rnd 2: Ch 1, 1 sc in same st, * work (1 sc in next sc, 2 sc in next sc). Rep around from *. Join with sl st.

Rnd 3: Ch 1, work 1 sc in same st, * work (1 sc in next 2 sc, 2 sc in next sc). Rep around from *. Join with sl st.

Rnd 4: Change to Color B. Ch 1, work 1 sc in same st, * work (1 sc in next 3 sc, 2 sc in next sc). Rep around from *. Join with sl st.

Rnd 5: Ch 1, work 1 sc in same st, * work (1 sc in next 4 sc, 2 sc in next sc). Rep around from *. Join with sl st.

Rnd 6: Ch 1, work 1 sc in same st, * work (1 sc in next 5 sc, 2 sc in next sc). Rep around from *. Join with sl st.

Rnd 7: Change to Color C. [Inc rnd].
Continue around circle with sc, increasing every 10th st, [2 sc in same st]. Join rows as done previously with sl st.

Rnd 8: Work 1 row of sc. Join with sl st.

Rep Rnds 7 and 8, changing colors every 4th row, keeping the red, gray, and black order. Work until you have 9 concentric circles, or until size desired. Fasten off.

Strap

Make ch 60 inches long. Join with sl st, ch 1, sc in each st, join at ch-1. Rep this until you have a band 2 inches wide.

Attach circles on each edge of band with sc, leaving an 8-inch opening, and continue to sc across open edges of bag.

Option

On 1 side, in middle of bag, ch 10 to form lp for button, make 10 sc in lp, continue across bag edge. Fasten off.

Check-Your-Stripes Sweater

This oversized sweater is made of 100% wool, but can also be made in cotton for spring and summer wear. It is an especially flattering style for any size, as it has a full, loose body, wide sleeves that can be pushed up or rolled, and a crew neck.

The colors of white and French blue in a bold checked and striped pattern make it an unusual and striking sweater that can be worn casually or dressed up. Designed by Robin Murray, it is quick and easy to make, all in a double crochet stitch.

While the directions are given for a small size, the finished project is meant to be oversized and measures 20 inches across. If you want to make it fit more snugly, adjust the stitches downward. The number of stitches for medium and large sizes are given in parenthesis.

Materials: Phildar Lenox wool yarn (3½-
oz. skeins)—4 skeins each in French blue
#13 and white #10
Yarn needle

Hook: H

Gauge:
15 sts = 4 inches
8 rows = 4 inches

DIRECTIONS

Sleeves: (make 2)
Using white yarn, make foundation ch of 48 (56, 64) sts and work in dc as follows: * 4 rows in white, 4 rows in blue *. Rep bet *'s 3 more times, until there are 8 stripes.

Gather sleeve edges tog by decreasing st number in half. For example: with white yarn, attach and pull lp through next 2 sts. Yo and pull through all 3 lps. * (Dec 2 sts to 1). Rep dec (*) around, then work 2 more rows, or desired length of sc to make cuff. Fasten off.

Back and Front: (same)
Using blue color make a foundation ch of 64 (72, 80) and work in dc as follows: * 4 rows in white, 4 rows in blue *. Rep bet *'s 3 times, until there are 8 stripes.

Make 1 st on either side with a colored thread to indicate position of armholes.

Checked Yoke: (make 2)
Row 1: Starting with white yarn, but carrying blue through, * work 4 dc with white, change to blue, and work 4 dc with blue *. Rep bet *'s across.

Row 2: Rep Row 1.

Row 3: Starting with * blue yarn, work 4 dc, then 4 dc with white *. Rep bet *'s across.

Row 4: Rep Row 3.
Rep these 4 rows 3 times. Fasten off.

FINISH

With right sides out, sc shoulder edges tog for 20 sts on either side. Sew sleeves to yoke with blunt yarn needle. With right sides of pieces tog, make small backstitches across fabric just below finished edges. Do not pull yarn too taut.

Another way to join the seams, especially for bulky yarn, is with a sl st.

Travel Slippers

Make a pair of slippers that fold easily into your suitcase or overnight bag. These warm slipons are wonderful for cold winter nights, whether you are traveling or staying at home. Designed by Anne Lane in a gray worsted, the front sports a design of a pink flower surrounded by a green border. This is a good way to use up your leftover yarn.

Materials: Knitting worsted weight yarn—
2 oz. in MC (gray), ½ oz. in Color A
(pink), ½ oz. in Color B (green)

Hook: 5 or F = small
6 or G = medium
7 or H = large

DIRECTIONS

Sole: (make 2)
With MC, ch 6, join with sl st to form ring.

Rnd 1: Ch 3 [counts as 1 dc], work 2 dc in ring, ch 2, * 3 dc, ch 2. Rep from * 2 times, join to top of ch-3 with sl st.

Rnd 2: Sl st to ch-2 sp, ch 3 [counts as 1 dc], dc, ch 2, 2 dc in ch-2 sp of preceding rnd, work 2 dc in each of next 2 dc, sk 1 dc, * work 2 dc, ch 2, 2 dc in next ch-2 sp, 2 dc in each of next 2 dc, sk next dc. Rep from * 2 times. Join to top of ch-3 with sl st.

Rnd 3: Sl st to ch-2 sp, ch 3 [counts as 1 dc], work 2 dc, ch 2, 3 dc in ch-2 sp, sk next dc, dc in next 7 dc, ch 1, dc in next ch-2 sp, sk 1 dc, work dc in next 7 dc, 3 dc, ch 2, 3 dc in next ch-2 sp, sk 1 dc, dc in next 7 dc, dc, ch 1, dc in next ch-2 sp, sk 1 dc, dc in next 7 dc. Join to top of ch-3 with sl st.

Rnd 4: Sl st to ch-2 sp, ch 3 [counts as dc], 2 dc, ch 2, 3 dc in ch-2 sp, work dc in next 10 dc, dc, ch 1, dc in ch-1 sp, dc in next 10 dc, work 3 dc, ch 2, 3 dc in ch-2 sp, dc in next 10 dc, dc, ch 1, dc in ch-1 sp, work dc in next 10 dc. Join to top of ch-3 with sl st.

Rnd 5: Rep Rnd 4, but with 13 dc bet corners.

Rnd 6: Rep Rnd 4, but with 16 dc bet corners.

Heel: (make 2)
With MC rep Rnds 1–3 of sole.

Toe: (make 2)
Using sole pattern, work Rnd 1 in Color A, Rnd 2 in Color B, and Rnd 3 in MC.

FINISH

With wrong sides tog, sew toe to front point of sole around all sides, leaving 2 dc, ch 2, 2 dc.

Sew heel to sole along back 2 sides only of diamond shape. Fasten off. Weave all yarn ends into underside of sts.

Short-Sleeved Sweater

A variegated blend of colors all in one yarn is perfect for a subtle multicolored sweater. The colors change without the problem of ending and attaching yarn when introducing a new color.

Worked on a large hook, this is a quick crochet project made in two pieces. While this is a short-sleeved sweater, you can easily extend the sleeves, if you wish. Simply continue to crochet until the sleeves are the length you'd like.

The directions are provided for a small size with medium and large in parenthesis. This is a boxy shape and the sizes run a little full. Keep this in mind when deciding which size to make.

Materials: Bernat Moire variegated yarn
   (50-gr. skeins)—10 skeins
Yarn needle

Hook: K

Gauge: 3 dc = 1 inch
3 rows = 2 inches

DIRECTIONS

Body
Make a ch of 84 (92, 100). Join with sl st.

Row 1: Ch 3 [first dc] and work 1 dc in each ch. Join with sl st. Continue making rows of dc until you have a tube 14 inches long (or desired length).

For back and sleeves, add-on row: Beg row with ch 3 and dc across. When you have half the dc, [42 (46, 50)], ch 17 and turn. Work 1 dc in 3rd ch from hook. Continue back to beg of that row

with 1 dc in each st, ending with ch 17. Work 1 dc in 3rd ch from hook.

Continue until you have reached a total of 11 (12, 13) rows of dc above the add-on row [or desired length to shoulder].

Front

On remaining sts, sk half of them and join the yarn with sl st. Ch 3, dc across, ch 17, and turn. Make 1 dc in 3rd ch from hook. Dc across row to middle where yarn was attached. Ch 3, turn, dc across. Continue until you have reached a total of 9 (11, 13) rows of dc.

Neck shaping: On next row, dc across 26 (28, 30), ch 3, turn, and dc across. Rep for other front side and sleeve, reversing directions. (Join yarn with sl st next to first line attachment).

FINISH

Sew shoulder edges and underarm edges tog.

Neck edge and ties: Ch 25, join at front neck opening, sc around neck, ch 25, and fasten off.

Kenya Bag

The colorful Kenya bags that have been so popular in recent years are easy to reproduce in colors to suit your wardrobe. Large and roomy, they make excellent totes for shopping. This one is made of cotton and is, therefore, washable. It is also softer than the originals, which are stiff and made of a ropelike material. The straps are woven fabric made for belts. They can be purchased from notions shops, in a matching color, by the yard.

The finished bag is 10 inches deep and measures 16 inches across.

Materials: Tahki Creole cotton twist (3½-
    oz. skeins)—1 skein each in Color A
    (blue), Color B (gray), Color C (mole),
    and Color D (violet)
5-foot length of 1-inch-wide woven strap

Hook: H

Gauge: 4 sc = 1 inch
4 rows = 1 inch

DIRECTIONS

Starting with Color C, ch 4. Join with sl st to form ring.

Rnd 1: Work 8 sc into ring.

Rnd 2: Work 2 sc in ring to join each sc [16 sc].

Rnd 3: Work (1 sc, 2 sc into next sc) 8 times [24 sc].

Rnd 4: Work (1 sc in 2 sts, 2 sc into next sc) 8 times [32 sc].

Rnd 5: Work (1 sc in 3 sc, 2 sc into next sc) 8 times [40 sc].

Rnd 6: Work (1 sc in 4 sc, 2 sc in next sc) 8 times [48 sc].

Rnd 7: Work (1 sc in 5 sc, 2 sc in next sc) 8 times [56 sts].

Rnd 8: Work (1 sc in 6 sc, 2 sc in next sc) 8 times [64 sts].

Rnd 9: Break off Color A. Attach Color B and work (1 sc in 7 sc, 2 sc into next sc) 8 times [72 sc]. Fasten off.

Rnd 10: Attach Color A and * sc around.

Rnds 11 and 12: Rep Rnd 10 from *. Fasten off.

Rnd 13: Attach Color D and sc in 8 sc, 2 sc into next sc around. Fasten off.

Rnd 14: Attach Color C and sc in 9 sc, 2 sc into sc all around. Fasten off.

Rnd 15: Attach Color B. * Sc around.

Rnds 16 and 17: Rep Rnd 15 from *. Fasten off.

Rnd 18: Attach Color A and sc 10, 2 sc in next sc around. [Last inc row. Next row starts basket side.] Fasten off.

Rnd 19: Continue working rnds of sc in color sequence as follows: 4 rnds in Color D, 1 rnd in Color B, 4 rnds in Color D, 1 rnd in Color A, 5 rnds in Color C, 3 rnds in Color A, 2 rnds in Color B, 1 rnd in Color D, 1 rnd in Color A, 1 rnd in Color D, 2 rnds in Color C, 1 rnd in Color B, 1 rnd in Color D, 1 rnd in Color B, 1 rnd in Color A, 1 rnd in Color B, 2 rnds in Color C, 4 rnds in Color A, and 2 rnds in Color D.

Fasten off.

FINISH

Divide strap material in half and cut 2 pieces. Place the bag flat on work surface and measure in 4 inches from each side edge. Pin each end of 1 strap inside bag at these points. Turn bag over and rep with 2nd handle. Stitch approximately 2 inches of strap to inside of bag.

Treasures for Tots

Babies are the most fun to handcraft for. The selection of yarns, colors, and projects is endless. Any new mother will love dressing her baby in a handmade sweater or layette for that memorable first outing.

Baby's needs are numerous, and so, you have lots from which to choose. A crib blanket of daisy squares will keep a baby snug and warm and will add to the charm of his or her room.

The variety of toys will delight babies, toddlers, and even teens. The flip-flop dolls, Red Riding Hood purse, and Bartholomew Rabbit are just a few.

Dress a newborn in the infant outfit and a toddler in the bulky-weight sweater and cap. Both will reflect your love and care and certainly bring compliments from friends.

All the projects in the children's section are made with washable yarns. The toys that have buttons for eyes and noses are secured with carpet thread for extra strength. However, for very young children, you might prefer to embroider facial features, thus avoiding the risk of buttons ending up in tiny mouths.

Toddler's Fall Sweater Set

Dress a toddler in a toasty warm sweater jacket and cap done in soft muted colors. The Tahki Ambrosia yarn is variegated, so you don't have to change yarns for a change of colors. One flows subtly into another.

These projects are easy to crochet and the finished garments will fit an average-size two-year-old. Directions in parentheses are for a four-year-old.

Materials: Tahki Ambrosia II bulky yarn
(4-oz skeins)—3 skeins in any color
4 wooden buttons

Hooks: I, J, and K

Gauge: (with K Hook)
5 hdc = 2 inches
4 rows = 2 inches

DIRECTIONS

The jacket is worked from the top down. Except where otherwise noted, each row ends with a ch 2, turn. If changing colors, drop the one you were using and work the ch-2 in a new color.

Jacket

With K hook, ch 39 (47). Hdc in 3rd ch from hook and each ch across [38 (46) hdc]. Ch 1, turn.

Row 1: Sc across.

Row 2: Work 8 (9) hdc, * 3 hdc in next st, 1 (2) hdc, 3 hdc in next st, 1 (2) hdc, 3 hdc in next st * [sleeve], 12 (14) hdc [back]. Rep bet *'s for sleeve, 8 (9) hdc [front], 50 (58) hdc. Ch 1, turn.

Row 3: Sc across.

Row 4: Work 9 (10) hdc, * 3 hdc in next st, 7 (9) hdc, 3 hdc in next st *, 14 (16) hdc, rep bet *'s for sleeve, 9 (10) hdc; [58 (66) hdc].

Row 5: Work 10 (11) hdc, * 3 hdc in next st, 9 (11) hdc, 3 hdc in next st *, 16 (18) hdc, rep bet *'s, 10 (11) hdc; [66 (74) hdc].

Row 6: Continue in inc pat, having 1 st more on fronts, 2 on back, and 2 bet each sleeve inc; [74 (84) hdc].

Row 7: Work across with incs; [82 (90) hdc].

Row 8: Rep Row 7 [90 (98) hdc].

Row 9: [Armhole row] Work 14 (16) hdc, ch 4 (6), sk next 19 (20) sts [sleeve], work hdc in next 24 (26) sts. Ch 4 (6), sk next 19 (20) hdc, 14 (16) hdc.

Rows 10–21: Work across in hdc.

Row 22: Work across in sc, continue in sc up front, around neck, and other front to beg. Work 3 sc in all corners. Join with sl st. Beg at top edge of front opening, work ch 2 for button lp. Rep with 2 inches between lps, ending at bottom edge.

Sleeves

Join to center of ch-4 (6). With K hook, work around with 1 hdc in each st and ch. Ch 2 and reverse work directions. Do this at end of each row. Work even for 6 (7) rnds. Change to J hook. Work even for 5 (7) rnds. Change to I hook. Work even for 6 rows. Work around in sc. Join with sl st. End off.

Sew buttons opposite lps on front of sweater.

Hat

Using K hook, ch 6. Join with sl st to form rnd.

Rnd 1: Work 6 sc in ring, 2 hdc in each sc. Join.

Rnd 2: Work 2 hdc in each sc. Join.

End each rnd with a ch-2 and reverse direction of work. Continue to inc 6 sts each rnd, until you have 48 sts. Work even in hdc for 10 rnds. Join with sl st. End off. Weave yarn ends into underside of hat.

Herb and Bernie Hand Puppets

This colorful pair brings delight to children of all ages. Made of cotton terry yarn, these hand puppets can also be used as wash cloths.

When making them for very young children, consider embroidering the eyes and nose, or securing the buttons with tightly knotted carpet thread.

Materials: Caron cotton terry (1¾-oz. skeins)—1 skein each in yellow, red, white, and black
4 eye buttons
2 round buttons for noses

Hook: H

DIRECTIONS
Starting at top and using yellow yarn, make a foundation ch of 4. Join with a sl st.

Herb (yellow face)
Rnd 1: Work 2 sc in each ch [8 sts]. Join with sl st, ch 1.

Rnd 2: Work 1 sc in each ch or st. Join with sl st, ch 1.

Rnd 3: * Work 2 sc in next st, 1 sc *. Rep bet *'s 3 more times [12 sts]. Join with sl st, ch 1.

Rnd 4: Rep Rnd 2.

Rnd 5: * Work 2 sc in next st, 2 sc *. Rep between *'s 3 more times [16 sts]. Join with sl st, ch 1.

Rnd 6: Rep Rnd 2.

Rnd 7: * Work 2 sc in next st, 3 sc *. Rep bet *'s 3 more times [20 sts]. Join with sl st, ch 1.

Rnd 8: Rep Rnd 2.

Rnd 9: * Work 2 sc in next st, 3 sc *. Rep bet *'s 4 more times [25 sts]. Join with sl st, ch 1.

Rnd 10: Rep Rnd 2.

Rnd 11: * Work 2 sc in next st, 4 sc *. Rep bet *'s 4 more times [30 sts]. Join with sl st, ch 1.

Rnd 12: Rep Rnd 2.

Rnd 13: * Work 2 sc in next st, 4 sc *. Rep bet *'s 5 more times [36 sts]. Join with sl st, ch 1.

Rnd 14: Work 21 sc, ch 14, sk 14 sc, 1 sc. Join with sl st, ch 1.

Rnd 15: Rep Rnd 2.

Rnd 16: Work rnd of sc with 6 decs spaced evenly around. Join with sl st, ch 1.

Rnd 17: Rep Rnd 2. Join with sl st. Fasten off.

Mouth

With red, make foundation ch of 6. Join with sl st.

Rnd 1: Work 1 sc in ch or st.

Rnd 2: Work 2 sc in st.

Rnd 3: * Work 2 sc in next st, 1 sc *. Rep bet *'s all around.

Rnd 4: * Work 2 sc in next st, 2 sc *. Rep bet *'s all around.

Rnd 5: * Work 2 sc in next st, 3 sc *. Rep between *'s all around.

Rnd 6: * Work 2 sc in next st, 4 sc *. Rep between *'s all around.
   With right sides tog, join mouth to opening with a sl st all around. Fasten off.

Body

Rnd 1: Using white yarn, work 1 sc around neck edge.

Rnd 2: With red yarn, work 1 dc around.
   Continue alternating Rnds 1 and 2 (5 more times) to make striped shirt. Fasten off.

Arms

Attach red yarn to first row of white on neck side. Ch 3 [first dc]. Work 3 dc in red dc, 1 dc in white. Ch 3, turn. Work dc across 3 times. Fasten off. With yellow, attach yarn in first dc. Insert hook in middle dc and work 6 dc to fan out for hand. Sl st in last dc. Fasten off.

Rep at other side for 2nd arm.

Ears

Attach yarn at 7th row from top on side of head. Sk 1 row of sc. Insert hook in next st and work 6 dc [same as hand]. Sk 1 sc row and sl st into next row. Fasten off.

Rep for other ear on other side.

FINISH

Attach black yarn to top of head. Sew on buttons for eyes and nose (or embroider).

Attach black yarn for eyebrows above button eyes.

Bernie (orange face)

Starting at top with orange yarn, make a foundation ch of 6. Join with sl st.

Rnd 1: Work 6 sc in ring. Join with sl st, ch 1.

Rnd 2: Work 2 sc in each sc [12 sts]. Join with sl st.

Rnd 3: * Work 2 sc in next sc, 1 sc *. Rep around bet *'s [18 sts]. Join with sl st.

Rnd 4: * Work 2 sc in next sc, 2 sc *. Rep around bet *'s [24 sts]. Join with sl st.

Rnd 5: * Work 2 sc in next sc, 3 sc *. Rep around bet *'s [30 sts]. Join with sl st.

Rnd 6: * Work 2 sc in next sc, 4 sc *. Rep around bet *'s [36 sts]. Join with sl st.

Rnd 7: * Work 2 sc in next sc, 5 sc *. Rep around bet *'s [40 sts]. Join with sl st.

Rnd 8: * Work 2 sc in next sc, 6 sc *. Rep around bet *'s [46 sts]. Join with sl st.

Rnd 9: Work 1 sc in each sc around.

Rnd 10: Rep Rnd 9.

Rnd 11: Work 28 sc, sk 18 sc, join with sl st.

Rnd 12: Sc in each sc. Join with sl st.

Rnd 13: Work rnd of sc with 6 decs spaced evenly around. Join with sl st.

Rnd 14: Rep Rnd 13.

Mouth

Follow same directions as for Herb through Rnd 6.

Rnd 7: * Work 2 sc in next sc, 5 sc. Rep from * around. Fasten off.

Body

Attach purple and work 2 rnds of dc. Attach white and work 1 rnd of dc. Attach yellow for 1 rnd of sc. Attach red and work 1 rnd of dc.

   Rep this sequence once more with an additional 2 rnds of purple dc at end. Fasten off.

FINISH

Make arms and ears same as for Herb. Attach hair, eyes, and nose.

Infant's Dress, Hat, and Booties

The matching set of dress, hat, and booties are made to fit a newborn to 6-month-old baby. This is also a project that you can make for a child's doll. The hat and yoke are made from granny squares easily stitched together. The hat and sleeves are ruffled around the edges and chain ties gather each sleeve and bootie top. The yarn is a soft acrylic that is machine washable.

Materials: Unger Roly Poly sport yarn
   (3½-oz. skeins)—2 skeins blue, 1 skein
   each in pink and white
Yarn needle

Hook: G

Gauge: 4½ rows = 2 inches
8 sts = 2 inches

DIRECTIONS

Booties: (make 2)
Using blue, ch 4, and join.

Rnd 1: Ch 1, 5 sc, join with sl st.

Rnd 2: Ch 1, 1 sc in same st, 2 sc in each st, join.

Rnd 3: Ch 1, * sc in next st, 2 sc in next st, rep from * around. Join.

Rnd 4: Ch 1, sc in each st around and join.

Rnds 5–10: Rep Rnd 4.

Rnd 11: Rep Rnd 4, but do not join. Ch 1 and turn work.

Rnd 12: Rep Rnd 11 9 times. Fasten off. Fold bootie in half and sew back edges [heel seam] tog.

Bootie Top

Rnd 1: Attach blue yarn, and ch 3. Dc around the opening and join.

Rnd 2: Ch 3, dc 2 in every st. Join and fasten off.

Ties

Using pink and white yarn tog, ch 40. Fasten off.

Beg and ending at Front, weave the ties through every 4th dc in Rnd 1 of bootie top. Tie in a bow at front.

Note: The hat and dress directions are given in infant size. For larger size (6 months–1 year), make the granny squares with 4 rnds instead of 3.

Hat: (make 4 squares)

Using pink yarn, ch 6 and join in ring with sl st into ch-1 sp.

Rnd 1: Using pink, ch 3, work 2 dc into ring, * ch 3, 3 dc into ring. Rep from * 2 times more, ch 3. Join with sl st to the 3rd of first ch-3. Fasten off.

Rnd 2: Join white yarn to any sp and ch 3, work (2 dc, ch 3, 3 dc) into same sp, * ch 1, work (3 dc, ch 3, 3 dc) into next sp. Rep from * 2 times more. Ch 1 and join with sl st to 3rd of first ch-3. Fasten off.

Rnd 3: Join blue yarn to ch-3 sp, ch 3, work (2 dc, ch 3, 3 dc) into same sp, * ch 1, work 3 dc into ch-1 sp, ch 1, work (3 dc, ch 3, 3 dc) into ch-3 sp. Rep from * 2 times more, ch 1, work 3 dc into ch-1 sp, ch 1. Join with a sl st to 3rd of first ch-3. Fasten off.

Rnd 4: (for larger size) Join blue yarn to ch-3 sp, ch 3, work (2 dc, ch 3, 3 dc) into same sp, * (ch 1, 3 dc into ch-1 sp) 2 times, ch 1, work (3 dc, ch 3, 3 dc) into ch-3 sp. Rep from * 2 times more, (ch 1, 3 dc into ch-1 sp) 2 times, ch 1, and join with sl st to 3rd of first ch-3. Fasten off.

FINISH

Follow Diagram and join squares with sc. With right sides up, join

HAT

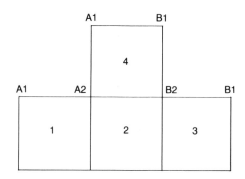

corners A-1 tog and sc along edge to point A-2. Fasten off. Rep for B-1 to B-2.

Ties

With blue yarn, ch 30. Sl st to hat at point C-1. Work 2 dc in each st around edge of hat to point C-2. Ch 30 and fasten off.

Dress: (yoke)

Make 4 granny squares as for hat, working 3 rnds for infant size, 4 rnds for larger size.

Refer to Diagram and, using blue yarn, join granny squares tog with sl st.

Starting with A to B to C, ch 5, sl st D to E to F, ch 5, and join G-1 and G-2.

Increase rnd: Ch 3 and work 2 dc in every st. Join.

Skirt

Ch 3, 1 dc in every st. Rep this row 12 times or desired length. Fasten off.

Border

Change to write yarn and attach to Skirt edge.

Rnd 1: Ch 3, 2 dc in attached st. * Ch 1, sk 2 dc, 3 dc in next st. Rep from * around. Join and fasten off.

Rnd 2: Using pink in ch-1 sp, ch 3, 2 dc, ch 1. * Work 3 dc in ch-1 sp, ch 1. Rep from * around. Join and fasten off.

DRESS

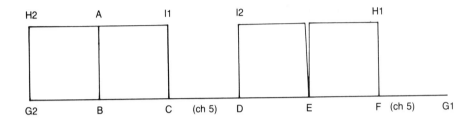

Rnd 3: Change to blue yarn and rep Rnd 2.

Rnd 4: Work 1 dc in each st. Fasten off.

Sleeves: (make 2)
Rnd 1: Attach blue yarn at Point 1 on granny square [shoulder]. Work 1 dc in each st along granny square edge to Point F. Continue to work 1 dc in each st of skirt ch-5. Continue up the other granny square edge from Point G-2 to H-2 and join.

Rnd 2: Work 1 dc in each st around.

Rnds 3–6: Rep Rnd 2.

Rnd 7: Work 2 dc in each st. Fasten off.
   Rep Rnds 1–7 for other sleeve.

Ties for Sleeves: (make 2)
Using pink and white yarn, ch 40. Beg at top of sleeve, weave ch through 4th dc of Rnd 6, and tie to make a bow. Rep on 2nd sleeve.

Tie for Dress Front
Using pink and white yarn, ch 50. Beg at top edge of front opening, weave ch through square edge, criss-crossing like a shoelace, and tie with a bow at neck.

Puppy Dog Toy

Make a colorful puppy dog to sit in the corner of your baby's crib or to give as a gift for a toddler. Made of acrylic yarn, this toy can be washed again and again and will still retain its shape. Keep in mind that the dog does not have to be made of realistic colors. A fantasy animal of bright reds and yellows will be just as adorable.

The finished size is 13 inches high. This is a good project for leftover yarns.

Materials: Knitting worsted weight yarn,
4-ply (4-oz. skeins)—2 skeins in Color
A (dark brown) and 1 skein in Color B
(reddish brown)
Large-eye darning needle
Small piece black felt
3 black buttons for eyes and nose
Small piece cardboard
Polyfil stuffing

Hook: G or size to give correct gauge

Gauge:
4 sc = 1 inch
4 rows = 1 inch

DIRECTIONS

Head: (center section)
Beg at lower edge of face with Color A. Ch 13 to measure approximately 3½ inches.

Row 1: Sc in 2nd ch from hook and in each ch across, ch 1, turn.

Row 2: Working on 12 sc, sc in each sc across, ch 1, turn.

Rep Row 2 until piece measures 13½ inches. Break and fasten off.

Side Section: (make 2)
Beg at top edge with Color B, ch 7 to measure approximately 1½ inches.

Row 1: Sc in 2nd ch from hook and in each ch across [6 sc], ch 1, turn.

Row 2: Work 2 sc in first sc, sc in each sc to within last sc, 2 sc in last sc [1 sc inc at each end], ch 1, turn.

Rows 3–6: Rep Row 2. Ch 1, turn.

Row 7: Working on 16 sc, sc in each sc across, ch 1, turn.
   Rep last row until piece measures approximately 4½ inches, ch 1, turn.

Next row: Draw up 1 lp in each of first 2 sc, yo hook, and draw through all 3 lps on hook, sc in each sc across to within last 2 sc, dec over last 2 sc [1 sc dec at each end], ch 1, turn.
   Rep last row 6 times [4 sc]. Break and fasten off.
   Fold center section in half crosswise, leaving last row of each side section and short edges of center section free at lower edge of head. Sew sides to center section, adjusting edges of center section to fit. Stuff firmly.

Body: (front)
Beg at lower edge with Color A, ch 30 to measure approximately 7½ inches.

Row 1: Sc in 2nd ch from hook and in each ch across, ch 1, turn.

Rows 2–4: Working on 29 sc, sc in each sc across, ch 1, turn.

Rows 5 and 6: Dec 1 sc at each end, sc in each sc across, ch 1, turn.

Rows 7 and 8: Working on 25 sc, sc in each sc across, ch 1, turn.
   Rep last 4 rows 5 times.

Rows 29 and 30: Working on 5 sc [neck edge], sc in each sc across. Break and fasten off.

Sides: (make 2)
Beg at lower edge with Color A, ch 25 to measure approximately 7 inches.

Row 1: Sc in 2nd ch from hook and in each ch across [24 sc], ch 1, turn.

Rows 2–8: Rep Rows 2–8 of front [20 sc]. Ch 1, turn.

Row 9: Dec 1 sc at each end, sc in each sc across, ch 1, turn.

Rows 10 and 11: Working on 18 sc, sc in each sc across, ch 1, turn.
   Rep last 3 rows 6 times, then rep Row 10 1 time [6 sc]. Break and fasten off.

Bottom

At front edge, with Color B, ch 29 to measure approximately 7½ inches.

Row 1: Sc in 2nd ch from hook and in each ch across [28 sc], ch 1, turn. Working in sc, dec 1 sc at each end on next row. Then rep dec every other row 12 times. Break and fasten off.

Tail

With Color A, ch 15 to measure approximately 4 inches. Having 14 sc on first row, work same as for bottom, dec 5 times instead of 13 times. Sew side edges tog. Stuff firmly.

Ears: (make 2)

Beg at lower edge with Color A, ch 9 to measure approximately 2¼ inches.

Row 1: Sc in 2nd ch from hook and in each ch across [8 sc], ch 1, turn.

Row 2: Work 2 sc in first sc [inc made], sc in each sc to within last sc, work 2 sc in last sc, ch 1, turn.
   Rep last row 2 times, ch 1, turn. Work on 14 sc until piece measures 3 inches. On next row, dec 1 st at each end, then rep dec every row, 3 times. Break and fasten off.

Pom-poms: (make 2)

Wind Color A 50 times around a 1½-inch piece of cardboard, slip lps off, and tie in center. Cut lps at each end and trim.

Finish

Using Color B and a large-eye darning needle, sew edges of sides to side edges of front section. Sew side sections tog for center back seam. Sew bottom to lower edge of body with beg ch towards front, and last row at back seam. Stuff firmly from top (neck) opening. Gather lower edge of head to fit top of body and sew head securely in place. Gather last row of each ear and sew 1 ear to each side of head ½ inch from center of side section. Tack back edge of each ear to head.

Legs: (make 4)
Beg at lower edge of front seams, pinch a section of body 1⅝ inches wide at bottom, tapering to nothing, about 4 inches above. With Color B, stitch tightly back and forth through all thicknesses of body for leg sections. At lower edge, sew 1 pom-pom to front of each leg. Sew tail to lower end of back seam.

Eyes
Cut 2 round felt circles. Sew these over seams at center of dog's face. Push stuffing in to get puffiness at lower section of face. Sew button over half of each eye circle.

Nose
Sew a button to center of face 1½ inches below top of button eyes.

Daisy Crib Blanket

Fresh as springtime, this overall daisy pattern is made up of familiar crocheted granny squares. This design is a favorite with most crocheters. You can create it as shown here, with a background of blue, or you might prefer to set your daisies in a field of green, as if growing on a lawn.

Made of four-ply washable Orlon, the finished afghan is 48 by 64 inches. You can, of course, alter the size by adding or subtracting motifs.

Materials: Coats & Clark Wintuk (3½-oz.)
skeins—5 skeins in Color A (yellow), 20
skeins in Color B (white), 20 skeins in
Color C (blue)

Hook: G

Gauge:
7 dc = 2 inches
Each motif = 4 inches square

DIRECTIONS
Granny Squares: (make 192)
With Color A, ch 4, join with sl st to form ring.

Rnd 1: Ch 3 [counts as 1 sc and ch 1], * sc in center of ring, ch 1, rep from * 4 times, join with sl st to 2nd ch of starting ch.

Rnd 2: * Work (sc, ch 1, sc) in next ch-1 sp, rep from * 5 times, join with sl st to first sc. Break off Color A.

Rnd 3: Attach Color B to any sc, ch 4, keeping last lp of each st on hook, work 2 dtr in same sc, yo and draw through 3 lps on hook, ch 3, * keeping last lp on each st on hook, work 3 dtr in next sc,

108

yo and draw through 4 lps on hook, ch 3, rep from * 10 times, join with sl st to tip of first petal [12 petals]. Break off Color B.

Rnd 4: Attach Color C to any ch-3 sp, ch 3 (3 dc, ch 2, 4 dc) in same sp [first corner], * work (4 dc in next ch-3 sp) 2 times, work (4 dc, ch 2, 4 dc) in next ch-3 sp, rep from *, work (4 dc in next 3-ch sp) 2 times, join with sl st to top of starting ch.

FINISH

With Color C, sew 12 motifs across and 16 down. With B, work 3 rnds of sc around afghan, working sc, ch 1, sc in corner sps. Join each rnd with sl st. Fasten off.

Bartholomew Rabbit and Toy Carrots

This oversized, overstuffed rabbit might have hopped right out of Mr. McGregor's garden after lunching in the cabbage patch. He's quite self-satisfied in his little blue breeches and is bursting out of his tweed jacket.

This is a soft toy that will delight a small child, as well as a teenager. Measuring 26 inches from the tip of his ears to the bottom of his feet, he is sure to win the hearts of all who take him into their homes. The clothes are removable, and you'll probably want to create an entire wardrobe to go with him.

Materials: Knitting worsted weight yarn
    (3½-oz. skeins)—3 skeins in white, 1
    skein in blue for pants
Any pink yarn, 2 ozs.
Bernat Pirandelle sport yarn, 3½ ozs. in claret color for sweater
4-ply knitting worsted in orange and green for carrot
1½ pounds polyfil stuffing
4 small buttons
Buttons for eyes, nose, and mouth

Hooks: H for rabbit and pants; F, G, and H
    for sweater

Gauge:
4 sc = 1 inch
9 rnds = 2 inches

DIRECTIONS

Body Back

Beg at center with white yarn, ch 10.

Rnd 1: Work 5 sc in 2nd ch from hook, sc in next 7 ch, 5 sc in last ch; working on opposite side of starting ch, sc in next 7 ch. Do not join rnds; mark end of rnds.

Rnd 2: Sc in each sc around [24 sc].

Rnd 3: Work (2 sc in each of next 5 sc, sc in next 7 sc) 2 times [34 sc].

Rnd 4: Sc in each sc around.

Rnds 5–14: On odd-numbered rnds, inc 5 sc evenly around each end. On even-numbered rnds, work even [84 sc]. End off. Fold oval in half lengthwise, mark center of 1 end for neck end.

Count over 5 sts to left of marker. Join yarn and work sc in each sc around to within 4 sts of marker. Fasten off. There should be 9 free sts at center for neck.

* Join yarn in first sc and work sc in each sc of last row. Rep from * 2 times more.

Body Front

Work as for body back. Sew front and back tog, leaving neck open. Stuff body firmly.

Head Front

Beg at center and ch 2.

Rnd 1: Work 6 sc in 2nd ch from hook. Do not join rnds; mark end of rnds.

Rnd 2: Work 2 sc in each sc around.

Rnd 3: Work (2 sc in next sc, sc in next sc) 6 times [18 sc].

Rnds 4–10: Continue working in rnds, inc 6 sc evenly each rnd, changing position of incs so they do not fall directly over previous incs [66 sc].

Rnds 11 and 12: Work even. At end of Rnd 12, sl st in next sc; do not end off. Ch 1, work 4 short rnds as for body, leaving 12 sts free for neck. Fasten off.

Head Back

Work as for front. Sew head pieces tog, leaving neck open. Stuff head firmly.

Legs: (make 2)

Using white yarn, beg at center of foot, ch 2. Work as for head through Rnd 3 [18 sc]. Work even in sc, until there are 24 rnds. Fasten off. Stuff legs and sew to body, about 2½ inches apart, centered over side seams of body.

Arms: (make 2)

Work as for legs, until 24 rnds of white are completed. Stuff arms and sew to body, about 1 inch below neck, centered over side seams of the body.

Ears: (make 2)

Using pink yarn, ch 16.

Rnd 1: Work 1 sc in 2nd ch from hook and 1 sc in each ch. Work 4 sc in each ch and continue back around, working sc in other side of foundation ch. Ch 1, turn.

Rnd 2: Work 1 sc in each of next 16 sc, ch 3, return working 1 sc in each sc on other side. Ch 1, turn.

Rnd 3: Work 1 sc in each of next 17 sc, 1 sc in ch-3 lp. Ch 3, 1 sc in ch-3 lp. Work 1 sc in each of next sc. Ch 1, turn.

Rnd 4: Rep Rnd 3, adding 1 more sc on each side. Fasten off.

   With white yarn, follow same directions as for pink ear, adding a 5th rnd same as Rnd 3, adding 1 more sc in each side.

   Do not fasten off. Place pink ear on white ear. With 1 row of sc around outside, connect ear pieces, easing in larger white side. Leave an 18-inch tail. Fold ear in half with pink on inside. Use 18-inch tail to overcast ear ends tog and attach to head with approximately 3 inches bet.

Sweater

Follow directions for Toddler's Fall Sweater on page 88. However, substitute F hook for K, G hook for J, and H hook for I. The yarn is a softer, finer texture, which further contributes to making the size small enough to fit rabbit.

Pants

Using H hook and blue yarn, ch 80. Join and work 4 rows for dc to form a tube.

Rows 5–8: Work in dc, but do not join row. Instead, turn and reverse work direction, making an opening for rabbit's tail. Join at end of 8 rows.

Fold tube in half, centering tail opening. St tog 8 middle sts for crotch seam. Attach yarn to leg openings and work 3 rows of dc joined to make pant legs.

Make a fat pom-pom tail and attach.

Carrot:

With F hook and beg with green, ch 2 (hdc, sc) 3 times in 2nd ch from hook. Join in first st. Ch 1. Join all rnds in this manner.

Rnd 2: Work (2 sc in next st, 2 hdc in next st) 6 times [12 sts]. Cut green.

Rnd 3: Join orange yarn. For this rnd only, work in back lps. (Sc in next st, 2 sc in next st) 6 times [18 sts].

Rnd 4: Work (1 sc in each of next 2 sts, 2 sc in next st) 6 times [24 sts].

Rnd 5: Work (1 sc in each of next 3 sts, 2 sc in next st) 6 times [30 sts].

Rnds 6–17: Work 1 sc in each st.

Rnd 18–24: Work (1 sc in each of next 3 sts, sk next st) 6 times [18 sts].

Rnds 25–31: Rep Rnd 6. Start stuffing on Rnd 25 and continue to stuff a little more as you finish each rnd.

Rnd 32: Sc in next st, sk next st, rep until opening is closed. Cut yarn leaving a tail 2½ inches for the "roots."

For the leaf section: Using green yarn, ch 15, sc in 2nd ch from hook. Ch 5, sl st in same st; *ch 7, sl st in next st; ch 3, sl st in next st; ch 5, sl st in next st; ch 7, sl st in next st; ch 4, sl st in next st; ch 6, sl st in next st; ch 3, sl st in next st; ch 5, sl st in next st; ch 6, sl st in next st; ch 4, sl st in next st; ch 5, sl st in next st; ch 3, sl st in next st; ch 4, sl st in last st *.

To make the stem: Ch 7, sl st in 2nd ch from hook and each of next 5 chs. Working on opposite side of original ch, rep bet *'s once. Cut yarn. Secure to center top of carrot.

Little Carrot

Beg with green yarn, ch 2, 6 hdc in 2nd ch from hook. Join. Cut yarn.

Rnd 2: Join orange yarn. This rnd only, work in back lps. Work 2 sc in each st. Join in first st. Ch 1. Join all rnds in this manner.

Rnds 3–30: Sc in each st. Stuff as you work.

Rnd 31: Sc in next st, sk next st all around.

Rnd 32: Sc in each st. Join. Cut yarn, leaving 2 inches for "roots."

To make the stem: Cut 6 8-inch lengths of green yarn. Fold in half and secure at center top of carrot.

Little Red Riding Hood Purse

Your favorite little girl will love carrying her very own Little Red Riding Hood purse. The doll is adorable when sitting on a bed or dresser, and the surprise is a zipper in the back of the skirt that opens to hold everything a little girl would want to carry. You will have fun making this precious toy complete with her own purse, lace apron, cape, and hood. She even has a carrying handle.

Materials: Knitting worsted weight yarn—
    2½ ozs. in red, ½ oz. in pale pink
Sport weight yarn—¼ oz. in brown
4 in. of pregathered 2-inch-wide eyelet lace
4-inch zipper
1-inch-diameter plastic ring
2 feet of ¼-inch-wide red ribbon
Small bunch of artificial flowers
Small amount of red and blue embroidery
    floss
Scrap of felt
Small amount of polyfil stuffing

Hooks: 00 aluminum and H

DIRECTIONS

Head
With size 00 hook and pink yarn, ch 2.

Rnd 1: Work 6 sc in 2nd ch from hook. Do not join rnds; carry a piece of contrasting color yarn between first and last st to mark beg of rnds.

Rnd 2: Inc in each sc around [12 sc].

Rnd 3: * Sc in first sc, inc in next sc. Rep from * around [18 sc].

Rnd 4: * Sc in first 2 sc, inc in next sc. Rep from * around [24 sc].

Rnds 5–9: Work even on 24 sc.

Rnd 10: Dec 6 sc evenly spaced around [18 sc].

Rnds 11–13: Continuing to work in sc, dec 6 sc evenly spaced in each rnd, stuffing head firmly before opening becomes too small. End off, leaving a 14-inch length of yarn.

Body

With 00 hook and red yarn, ch 6. Join with sl st to form ring.

Rnd 1: Work 12 sc in ring. Do not join rnds. Mark as for head.

Rnd 2: * Sc in first sc, inc in next sc. Rep from * around [18 sc].

Rnd 3: * Sc in first 2 sc, inc in next sc. Rep from * around [24 sc].

Rnds 4–9: Work even on 24 sc.

Rnd 10: Sc in each sc around, keeping work very loose.

Rnd 11: [Work in back lps only] * Sc in first 2 sc, dec over next 2 sc. Rep from * around [18 sc].

Rnd 12: [Work through both lps] * Sc in first sc, dec over next 2 sc. Rep from * around [12 sc]. Stuff body firmly before opening becomes too small.

Rnd 13: [Work through both lps] * Dec over first 2 sc. Rep from * around [6 sc]. End off, leaving a 6-inch length of yarn. With yarn needle, gather remaining sts tog and fasten firmly.

Skirt

With 00 hook and red yarn, join yarn to the front lps of Rnd 10 of body.

Row 1: Ch 3 in first lp. In same sp make 1 hdc, * in next lp make 2 hdc. Rep from * around [48 hdc]. Ch 3, turn.

Rows 2–8: Make 1 hdc in each hdc across. Ch 3 and turn at end of each row.

Rows 9–10: Make 1 hdc in each hdc around, joining first and last hdc to top of ch-3 with sl st. End off at end of Row 10.

Purse Bottom

Using size H hook and red yarn, ch 2.

Rnd 1: Work 6 sc in 2nd ch from hook. Do not join rnds. Mark as for head.

Rnd 2: Inc in each sc around [12 sc].

Rnd 3: * Sc in first sc, inc in next sc. Rep from * around [18 sc].

Rnd 4: * Sc in first 2 sc, inc in next sc. Rep from * around [24 sc].

Rnds 5–8: Working in sc, continue to inc 6 sc evenly spaced around [48 sc in Rnd 8]. End off, leaving a 14-inch length of yarn. Sew purse bottom to last row of skirt with neat overcast sts.

Arms: (make 2)
Using size 00 hook and pink yarn, ch 2.

Rnd 1: Work 6 sc in 2nd ch from hook. Do not join rnds. Mark as for head.

Rnd 2: Inc in first sc, sc in each of next 5 sc [7 sc].

Rnd 3: Sc in first 3 sc, inc in next sc, sc in last 3 sc [8 sc]. End off pink and attach red yarn.

Rnd 4: With red color, sc in first 7 sc, inc in last sc [9 sc].

Rnds 5–10: Work even on 9 sc.

Rnd 11: Sc in first 5 sc, ch 1 and turn, sc in same 5 sc. End off, stuff firmly and sew across Rnd 10.

Hood and Cape
Using size 00 hook and red yarn, ch 2.

Row 1: Dc in 3rd ch from hook and in each ch across [20 dc]. Ch 3, and turn.

Rows 2–6: Work even on 20 dc, ch 3, and turn at end of each row. At end of Row 6, fasten off, leaving 8-inch length of yarn. Join pink yarn to other side of starting ch.

Row 1 (beading row): * Ch 4, sk next ch, dc in next ch sp, ch 1. Rep from * across, ending ch 1, dc in last sp [10 sps], ch 3, and turn.

Row 2: Inc in each dc and ch-1 sp across [40 dc]. Ch 3 and turn.

Rows 3–5: Dc in each dc across, ch 3, and turn at end of each row. Fasten off at end of Row 5.

Fold hood in half and sew along top edge with neat overcast sts. Run an 8-inch length of ribbon through beading row.

Ring of Carrying Strap

Using size 00 hook and pink yarn, sc around in the 1-inch-diameter plastic ring until it is completely covered. Fasten off, leaving a 14-inch length of yarn.

Carrying Strap

Using size 00 hook and red yarn, ch 51, sc in 2nd ch from hook and in each ch across. Fasten off, leaving a 10-inch length of yarn.

FINISH

1. Sew the head firmly to body.

2. Cut 24 pieces of brown sport-weight yarn 8 inches long. Sew them with a backstitch to top and back of head. Gather ends and tie in a bunch at nape of neck.

3. Using a backhand st, sew zipper in skirt opening, bringing top of zipper to top of skirt opening.

4. Hem sides of eyelet and sew a piece of ribbon across top edge to create equal ties on each side of eyelet apron.

5. Tack top of apron to doll's waist and tie in a bow at back.

6. Put hood over head. Tie ribbons around neck in a bow.

7. Sew ring firmly to back of head through hood and hair. Sew strap ends tog through ring.

8. Cut 2 pieces of felt each 1½ by 1½ inches. Place 1 on top of the other and clip bottom corners so they curve to form a purse shape. Sew tog on 3 sides with a blanket stitch, leaving the top open. Cut a narrow 2-inch-long strip of felt and attach it to center of either side of basket to form the handles. Place a small bunch of flowers in basket and sew firmly in place.

9. Using red floss, embroider a smiling face. Use blue for round eyes.

Goldilocks and Mama Bear Flip-Flop Dolls

Anne Lane has designed a charming flip-flop doll that is a two-in-one creation. At first, it appears to be Goldilocks with her pretty yellow curls and long blue lace-trimmed dress. Turn her upside down, flip the skirt over her head, and Mama Bear appears in a long pink gown.

This is an adorable toy, soft and cuddly, for any small child.

Materials: Knitting worsted weight yarn—
½ oz. each in pale pink (MC for Mama Bear) and bright yellow, 1 oz. in dark brown, 2 ozs. each in blue (MC for Goldilocks) and deep pink
10 yds. of white yarn
6 in. of pregathered 1-inch-wide eyelet lace
6 in. of rosebud or lace trim
Small amounts of red and black embroidery floss
4 ¼-inch-diameter wiggle eyes
Carpet thread for securing eyes
Polyfil stuffing

Hooks: F and H

DIRECTIONS
Make 2 of the basic pattern, using colors specified for each half of doll.

Head
Using F hook and brown yarn for Mama Bear, or pale pink for Goldilocks, start at top of head and ch 2.

Rnd 1: Work 6 sc in 2nd ch from hook. Do not join rnds. Carry a piece of contrasting color yarn bet first and last sc to mark beg of rnds.

Rnd 2: Inc in each sc around [12 sc].

Rnd 3: * Sc in first sc, inc in next sc. Rep from * around [18 sc].

Rnd 4: * Sc in first 2 sc, inc in next sc. Rep from * around [24 sc].

Rnd 5: * Sc in first 3 sc, inc in next sc. Rep from * around [30 sc].

Rnds 6–12: Work even on 30 sc.

Rnd 13: Dec 15 sc evenly spaced around.
   Stuff head firmly before opening becomes too small.

Rnd 14: Dec 7 sc in first 14 sc, sc in last sc [8 sc].

Rnd 15: Work even on 8 sc. End off and join the MC.

Body
Rnd 16: Sc in first sc, inc in each of remaining 7 sc [15 sc].

Rnd 17: Inc in each sc around [30 sc].

Rnds 18–27: Work even on 30 sc. [*Note:* Work Rnd 27 very loosely.]

Skirt
Before starting Rnd 28, change to size H hook.

Rnd 28: Work in front lps only and ch 3 [counts as 1 dc], dc in same lp. * Work 2 dc in next lp. Rep from * around [60 dc]. Join to top of ch-3 with a sl st.

Rnd 29: Work through both lps and ch 3 [counts as 1 dc], dc in remaining 59 dc [60 dc total]. Join to top of ch-3 with a sl st.

Rnds 30–37: Rep Rnd 29. Fasten off at end of Rnd 37.

Assembly
Stuff bodies firmly and sew tog through back lps of Rnd 27.

Skirt Edging
Using white yarn and size F hook, join yarn to back lps of skirts.

Edging round: Work in back lps only and ch 3 [counts as 1 dc], dc through same 2 lps [1 lp from each skirt]. Ch 2 and 2 dc in same lps. * Sk 2 dc of both skirts. In back lps of next dc [1 lp from each skirt] make 2 dc, ch 2, 2 dc. Rep from * around [20 shells made]. Join to top of ch-3 with sl st. Fasten off.

Arms

Make 2 with pale pink yarn and 2 with brown yarn for each half of doll.

With F hook and specified yarn color, start at tip of the arm and ch 2.

Rnd 1: Work 6 sc in 2nd ch from hook. Do not join rnds. Mark as for head.

Rnd 2: * Work sc in first sc, inc in next sc. Rep from * around [9 sc].

Rnd 3: Work even on 9 sc.

Rnd 4: Dec 3 sc evenly spaced around [6 sc]. End off arm color and join MC (blue or deep pink).

Rnd 5: Work even on 6 sc.

Rnd 6: Inc 3 sc evenly spaced around [9 sc].

Rnds 7–14: Work even on 9 sc. Fasten off at end of Rnd 14, leaving an 8-inch length of yarn for sewing.

Stuff arm firmly, sew ends tog, and st arm to body.

GOLDILOCKS FINISH

1. With yarn needle and 18-inch lengths of doubled yellow yarn, make small lps all over top and back of head for hair.

2. Sew or paste on eyes.

3. With red embroidery floss, make a smiling mouth.

4. Sew eyelet lace around neck for collar.

You can add more details if desired, such as an eyelet apron, small pearl buttons to the bodice, and a ribbon bow in the hair.

Mama Bear's Ears: (make 2)

Using size F hook and brown yarn, start at inside of ear and ch 2.

Row 1: Make 5 sc in 2nd ch from hook. Ch 1 and turn.

Row 2: Inc in each sc [10 sc]. Ch 1 and turn.

Row 3: Sl st in each sc across. End off, leaving an 8-inch length of yarn for sewing.

Mama Bear's Face
Using F hook and brown yarn, ch 3.

Row 1: Sc in 2nd and 3rd ch from hook. Ch 1 and turn.

Row 2: Inc in each sc [4 sc]. Ch 1 and turn.

Row 3: Work even on 4 sc. Ch 1 and turn.

Row 4: Sc in first sc, inc in each of next 2 sc, sc in last sc [6 sc]. Ch 1 and turn.

Rows 5–8: Work even on 6 sc. Ch 1 and turn at end of each row.

Row 9: Sc in first sc, dec 2 sc over next 4 sc, sc in last sc [4 sc]. Ch 1 and turn.

Row 10: Work even on 4 sc. Ch 1 and turn.

Row 11: Dec 2 sc over the 4 sc [2 sc]. Ch 1 and turn.

Row 12: Work even on 2 sc. Fasten off, leaving a 12-inch length of yarn for sewing.

MAMA BEAR'S FINISH

1. Sew face to front of head so it is centered on lower part. Stuff face firmly before it is completely attached.

2. Sew ears to each side of head.

3. Sew or paste on eyes.

4. Use black embroidery floss to sew on a nose and smiling mouth on point of face.

Bumblebee Poncho Puppet

A bumblebee poncho puppet made of black and yellow stripes of yarn is a perfect rainy-day toy. Any child will love this make-believe "yarnimal" from Anne Lane. (See Source List for more designs.)

Materials: Sport yarn—2 ozs. each black
    and yellow—1 oz. in white
3-inch-diameter Styrofoam ball
¾-inch-wide piece of cardboard
12 inches of ¼-inch-wide yellow ribbon
Small amount of red embroidery floss
2 6-inch black chenille pipe cleaners
2 ½-inch wiggle-eye buttons
Carpet thread

Hook: F or #5 aluminum or plastic

DIRECTIONS
Using black yarn and starting at top of head, ch 2.

Basic Pattern
Work head [Rnds 1–21] and yoke of poncho [Rnds 22–26] in a pat of 1 rnd black, 2 rnds yellow. Work poncho [Rnds 27–32] in alternate rnds of black and yellow, starting with black on Rnd 27.

Rnd 1: Work 6 sc in 2nd ch from hook. Do not join rnds. Carry a piece of contrasting color yarn bet first and last sc to mark beg of rnds.

Rnd 2: Inc in each sc around [12 sc].

Rnd 3: * Sc in first sc, inc in next sc. Rep from * around [18 sc].

Rnds 4–6: Continuing to work in sc, inc 6 sc, evenly spaced in each rnd [36 sc in Rnd 6].

Rnds 7–14: Work even on 36 sc.

Rnds 15–18: On Rnd 15 insert Styrofoam ball. Working around ball, dec 6 sc, evenly spaced in each rnd [12 sc in Rnd 18].

Rnds 19–20: Work even on 12 sc.

Rnd 21: Inc in each sc around [24 sc].

Yoke

Rnds 22–24: Inc 6 sc evenly spaced in each rnd [42 sc in Rnd 24].

Rnds 25–26: Inc 3 sc evenly spaced in each rnd [48 sc in Rnd 26].

Body of Poncho

Caution: Pay special attention to Rnd 27. It must be followed exactly, as it sets the pattern for the entire body of the poncho.

Rnd 27: Ch 3 [counts as 1 dc], 2 dc, ch 2, 3 dc in same sc, ch 1 [first corner shell made]. * Sk 2 sc, 3 dc in next sc, ch 1 [plain shell made]. Rep from * 2 times, sk 2 sc, 3 dc in next sc, ch 2, 3 dc in same sc, ch 1 [2nd corner shell made]. * Sk 2 sc, 3 dc in next sc, ch 1. Rep from * 2 times, sk 2 sc, 3 dc in next sc, ch 2, 3 dc in same sc, ch 1 [3rd corner shell made]. * Sk 2 sc, 3 dc in next sc, ch 1.

Rep from * 2 times, sk 2 sc, 3 dc in next sc, ch 2, 3 dc in same sc, ch 1 [4th corner shell made]. * Sk 2 sc, 3 dc in next sc, ch 1. Rep from * 2 times, sk 2 sc and join to top of first ch-3 with a sl st. Sl st to center of ch-2 sp.

Rnds 28–32: For each of these rnds, follow pat given in Rnd 27, making plain shells in each ch-1 sp and corner shells in each ch-2 sp. [*For each succeeding rnd there will be 1 more plain shell bet each pair of corner shells, or 4 more plain shells on each rnd.*] End off neatly.

FINISH

1. Wrap white yarn around cardboard 164 times. Cut through lps on 1 side and use these pieces to knot each 1 around edge of poncho to create a fringe. Trim evenly all around.

2. Use a knife to hollow out a hole in Styrofoam ball inside poncho, so that a finger can fit inside.

3. Fold poncho in a triangle, and, using yellow ribbon, tie a bow through both layers, 2 shell rows down from neck and 4 shell rows in from edge on each side. This forms the "arms."

4. Using carpet thread, sew eyes firmly in place on head, with approximately 1¼ inches between.

5. Use red embroidery floss to stitch a smiling mouth.

6. Push each of chenille sticks 3 inches into top of head, 1 on each side, 5 rnds down from top. They should stick out at an angle from head. Curl ends slightly.

Baby's Carriage or Crib Coverlet

There is nothing like the arrival of a new baby to inspire some handmade projects. What better excuse is there a carriage cover or receiving blanket than to welcome a friend's newborn? The pretty turquoise yarn contrasts nicely with white for an easy-to-crochet granny square cover. This one fits a carriage, but, if you want to make it crib size, simply add more squares. The finished size with the border is 18 by 25 inches, and it is completely washable.

Materials: Caron Soft N Easy 4-ply yarn (3½-oz. skeins)—2 skeins in Color A (white), 1 skein in Color B (soft turquoise)
Yarn needle

Hook: F

Gauge:
Each square = 3½ inches

DIRECTIONS

Granny Squares: (make 35)
With Color B, ch 4 and join with sl st to form ring.

Rnd 1: Ch 3 [counts as first dc], dc in ring, (ch 3, 3 dc in ring) 3 times, ch 3, dc in ring, join with sl st to top of ch-3. Fasten off. Join Color A to top of ch-3.

Rnd 2: Ch 4, sk 1 dc, work dc in next dc, ch 1, sk 1, dc, (in ch-3 sp work dc, ch 1, dc, ch 1, dc [corner], ch 1, sk 1 dc, work dc in next dc, ch 1, sk 1 dc) 4 times. Ch 1, join with sl st to 3rd ch of ch-4.

Rnd 3: Ch 4, * work dc in next dc, dc in next dc, ch 1, in next dc, work corner, (ch 1, dc in next dc) 3 times. Ch 1, dc in next dc, ch 1, rep from * 2 times. In next dc, work corner, ch 1, join with sl st to 3rd ch of ch-4.

Rnd 4: Ch 4, (dc in next dc, ch 1) 3 times, * work corner, (ch 1, dc in next dc) 5 times, ch 1, rep from * 2 times, work corner, ch 1, dc in next dc, ch 1, sl st in top of ch-4. Fasten off.

Joining

Arrange squares as shown in Diagram, 5 across and 7 down. Sc squares tog from wrong side, working 1 sc through each pair of corresponding dc, picking up back lps of dc only, and working 1 sc in corner sps.

Edging

Attach Color A in a ch-1 sp.

Rnd 1: Ch 2 [first dc], dc in same sp, 2 dc in next ch-1 sp, * (ch 1, 2 dc in next 2 ch-1 sps). Rep from * all around. At corners, work 2 dc, 1 ch, 2 dc, in one ch-1 sp. Join in top of ch-2.

Rnd 2: Ch 3, 2 dc, ch 2, 3 dc [shell] in each ch-1 sp to corners.

Corners: Work 2 shells in each ch-1 sp. Join at top of ch-3.

Rnd 3: (Ch 5, sc) in each sc-sp around. In corners, sc, ch 5, sc in same sp to make lp. Join.

Rnd 4: In each ch-5 sp, work 2 sc, 3 ch, 2 sc around.
  Continue around and fasten off.

Bazaar Best-Sellers

Bazaar time is a terrific excuse to begin crafting. Crocheted projects always sell well, and most people who participate agree that it is important to keep the items small because they can be priced to sell and it is possible to make them in multiples. Such is the case with Christmas ornaments.

Two ladies who are real pros in this area are Sally George of Oregon and Anne Lane from Massachusetts. They have been designing and selling crochet patterns for years. Most of their customers make the projects for bazaar sales. Sally says that the Christmas angel, for which she has provided the pattern, is her most popular, second only to her snowflakes.

Who could resist the pixie in Santa's boot or a strawberry closet sachet? It not only smells good, but it looks bright and cheerful hanging anywhere. The little gift cards are easy to make in multiples, and each one can be unique. This is a good way to use up all that leftover scrap yarn.

So have fun creating a bunch of gifts for Christmas to sell at a fund raiser or just for the sheer enjoyment of it.

Christmas Angel

Make this darling crocheted angel with brown hair and a golden halo for the top of your Christmas tree or as an ornament. It is sure to be a hit at your next bazaar as well, so make plenty.

Materials: Knitting worsted weight 4-ply
yarn—small amounts in pale pink, yellow, brown, and white
Embroidery floss in blue or brown for eyes
Floss in red for mouth
Polyfil stuffing
Yarn needle

Hook: G

Gauge:
4 sc = 1 inch
4½ sc rows = 1 inch

DIRECTIONS

Head
Starting at top, with pink yarn and G hook, ch 2.

Rnd 1: Work 6 sc in 2nd ch from hook, do not join, but mark rnds with yarn of contrasting color.

Rnd 2: Work 2 sc in each sc around [12 sc].

Rnd 3: Work (1 sc in next sc, 2 sc in next sc) 6 times [18 sc].

Rnds 4–6: Work sc in each sc. Beg stuffing with polyfil stuffing.

Rnd 7: Work (1 sc in next sc, 1 dec in next 2 sc) 6 times [12 sc].

Rnd 8: (Dec in next 2 sc) 6 times, sl st to next sc. Fasten off.

Arms: (make 2)

Using pink yarn, ch 8. Sc in 2nd ch from hook and each of next 5 ch, 3 sc in end ch. Working along other side of ch, sc in each ch. Break off, leaving 6 inches of yarn for sewing.

Fold piece in half lengthwise and sew sides tog with overcast st, catching the outside lps. By pulling sts slightly, you can make arm curve. For bendable arms, put a pipe cleaner in before sewing.

Halo

Using yellow yarn, ch 25 tightly (for 5 inches). Join, leaving 3 inches to sew with.

Wings: (make 2)

Using yellow yarn, ch 13.

Row 1: Sl st in 2nd ch from hook, sc in each of next 3 ch, work 2 sc in next ch, sc in next ch, dc in next ch, ch 1, holding back last lp of each st, dc in each of next 4 ch [5 lps on hook], yo and through all 5 lps for cl, dc in last ch, ch 1, and turn.

Row 2: Work 1 sc in dc, sc in top of cl, sk ch, sc in dc, sc in next sc, 2 sc, sl st in next sc, ch 1 and turn.

Row 3: Sk sl st, sl st in sc, sc in next sc, 2 sc in next sc, sc in each of next 3 sc, 2 sc in next sc, 2 sc in last sc, 2 sc in first part of pc st of dc, sl st in next part of dc pc st, join to beg ch and fasten off, leaving 3 inches of yarn for sewing.

Dress

[Note: When working rnds in sc that are joined with a sl st, always work first sc into same sc that is sl st'd into or the joining st. In that way, at end of each rnd, all sl sts line up on top of each other and are neither counted nor worked into.]

Using white and starting at top, ch 8, join to form ring and ch 1.

Rnd 1: Sc in each ch, join, ch 1 [8 sc].

Rnd 2: Sc in each sc around. Join, ch 1.

Rnd 3: Sc in first 2 sc, 2 sc in next sc, sc in each of next 3 sc, 2 sc in next sc, sc in last sc. Join, ch 1 [10 sc].

Rnd 4: Sc in first 2 sc, 2 sc in next sc, sc in each of next 4 sc, 2 sc in next sc, sc in last 2 sc, join, ch 1 [12 sc].

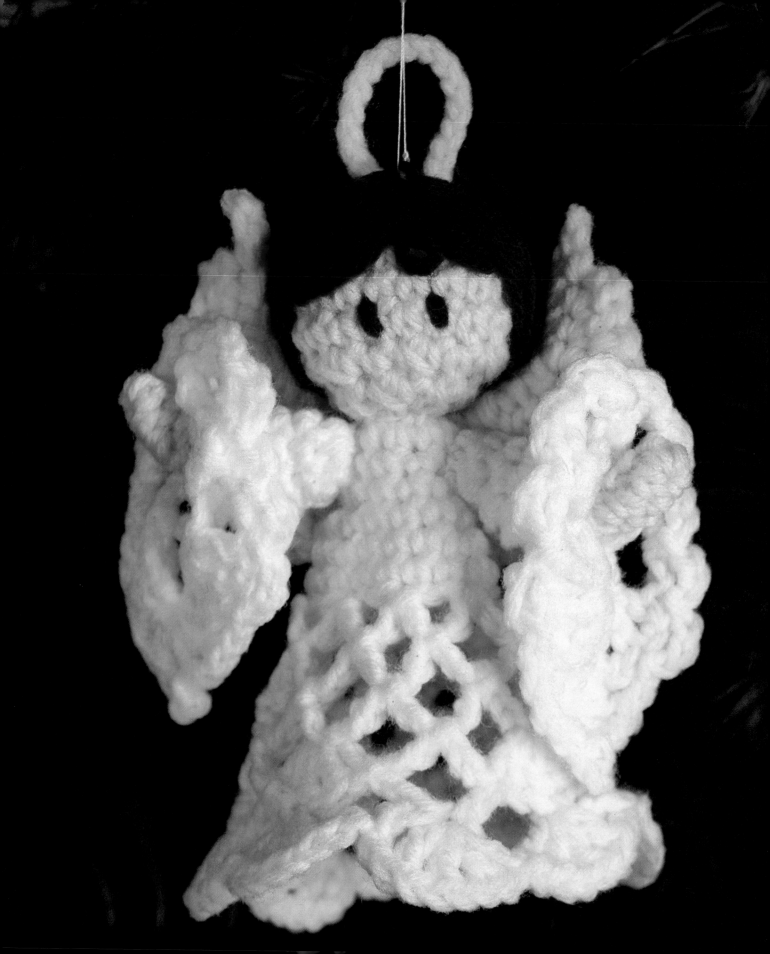

Rnd 5: Sc in first 3 sc, 2 sc in next sc, sc in each of next 4 sc, 2 sc in next sc, sc in last 3 sc. Join, ch 1 [14 sc].

Rnd 6: Work 2 sc in first sc, sc in rest of sc around. Join [15 sc].

Rnd 7: (Ch 4, sk 1 sc, sl st in next sc) 7 times, ch 2, dc in joining st [8 lps].

Rnds 8–10: (Ch 5, sl st in next lp) 7 times, ch 3, dc in dc that joined previous rnd.

Rnd 11: Work 3 dc in same dc just worked into, sl st in next lp making shell (ch 5, sl st in next lp, 3 dc in sl st bet next 2 lps, sl st in next lp) 3 times, ch 3, dc in first dc of shell [4 lps and 4 shells].

Rnd 12: (Ch 5, sl st in top of shell, ch 5, sl st in next lp) 3 times, ch 5, sl st into shell, ch 3, dc in dc of previous rnd [8 lps].

Rnd 13: (Ch 1, dc) 3 times in same dc just worked into, ch 1, sl st in next lp, * (ch 1, dc) 3 times in sl st bet next 2 lps, ch 1, sl st to next lp, rep from * around, join to first shell. Fasten off.

Sleeve
Using same color yarn, ch 2.

Rnd 1: Work 6 sc in 2nd ch from hook, join, ch 1 [6 sc].

Rnds 2–3: Sc in each sc around. Join and ch 1.

Rnd 4: Work (sc in next 2 sc, 2 sc in next sc) 2 times. Join, ch 1 [8 sc].

Rnd 5: Work (1 sc in each of next 3 sc, 2 sc in next sc) 2 times. Join [10 sc].

Rnd 6: Ch 4, sk joining st and next sc, sl st in next sc (ch 4, sk next sc, sl st in next sc) 3 times, ch 2, dc sl st.

Rnd 7: (Ch 5, sl st in next lp) 4 times, ch 3, dc in dc joining previous rnd.

Rnd 8: * (Ch 1, dc) 2 times in st bet lps, ch 1, sl st to next lp, rep from * only once, making 2 shells, ch 3, and turn.

Rnd 9: Sk ch 1, sl st in next dc (ch 1, dc) 2 times in sl st bet shells, ch 3, sl st in 3rd ch from hook for pc, (dc, ch 1) 2 times in same st as dc's made before pc, sl st to center dc in next shell, ch 3, sl

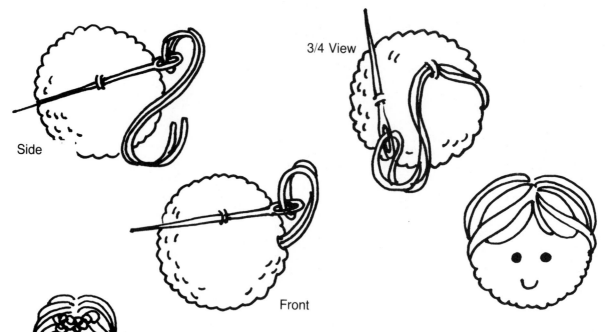

Side

3/4 View

Front

st in next dc, (ch 3, sl st in lp, ch 3, sl st in sl st) 3 times, ch 3, sl st in lp, end off.

FINISH

With dress yarn, sew head to neck of dress. Place arms in sleeves, so hands show at edges. Sew in place with dress yarn. Sew sleeve at "shoulder" of dress, taking sts in top 3 rnds of dress. With yellow, sew on wings. Pull down on skirt on 1 side to make angel "fly."

Add hair with brown or black yarn; place halo on top of hair with sl st in back. Tack only in that place so the halo will float over head. Embroider features on face. Make a hanging lp out of sewing thread and attach to top of head.

Keep embroidery of face simple. Use French knots in yarn for eyes. Use stem stitch with floss for mouth.

For hair, thread yarn needle so strand of yarn is doubled. Take long sts from 1 side of head (A) to other side (C), going under a sc at top center of head (B) [where the part would be]. Continue in this manner until entire head is covered.

Snowflake Tree Ornaments

The snowflake patterns provided here are as unique as the real things. The delicate lacy designs look wonderful on a Christmas tree and are always a bazaar best-seller.

Sometimes I like them soft and unstarched, but the stiffly starched snowflakes hang beautifully and will keep for years and years. Each one presented here is of a different size and I think you will want to make all of them. The basic snowflake is approximately 4½ inches across.

Materials for Basic Snowflake: Coats & Clark Speed Cro-Sheen cotton yarn—1 ball in white

Hook: #6 steel

Materials for Starching and Blocking:
Sheet of Styrofoam
Typing paper
Plastic wrap
Masking tape
Rustproof copper pins
Paper towels
Waterproof pen
Stiffening agents:

Stif'n Fab®: Available in craft stores or directly from dealer. (See Source List.) Dries rapidly and is water-soluble for easy cleanup and future laundering. Shake, pour into a small bowl, and soak snowflakes.

Dry starch: Mix and cook a heavy solution as directed on the box. Allow to cool. Premixed liquid and spray starches don't give enough body.

Sugar: Heat ½ cup water with ¾ cup sugar until sugar dissolves. Allow to cool.

DIRECTIONS FOR BASIC SNOWFLAKE

Ch 4, join with sl st to form ring, ch 3.

Rnd 1: Work 11 dc into ring, join at top of ch-3.

Rnd 2: Ch 3, 2 dc in same st, ch 2, sk 1 dc, * 3 dc in next dc, ch 2, sk 1 dc, rep from * around, and join.

Rnd 3: Ch 3, 1 dc in same st, 3 dc in next dc, 2 dc in next dc, * 2 dc in next dc, 3 dc in next dc, 2 dc in next dc, rep from * around, join.

Rnd 4: * Ch 3, sl st in same st, ch 7, sl st in 4th ch from hook, dc in each of next 5 dc, holding the last lps of each dc on hook until there are 6 lps on hook, yo and through all 6 lps (ch 5, sl st in 4th ch from hook for pc) 4 times, sl st into base of 3rd pc from hook, ch 5, sl st in 4th ch from hook, sl st into base of next pc, ch 5, sl st in 4th ch from hook, sl st into top of cl of dcs, ch 3, sl st into next dc, ch 3, sl st in same st, ch 5, sl st into 4th ch from hook, ch 1, sl st into next dc, rep from * around, join, end off.

DIRECTIONS FOR VARIATION SNOWFLAKES

Snowflake 1: (approximately 3¼ inches across)

Starting at center, ch 6, join with sl st to form ring.

Rnd 1: Ch 3, into ring work 1 dc, ch 1, * work 2 dc, ch 1, rep from * 4 times, join to top of ch-3.

Rnd 2: Ch 3, 1 dc in same st, 2 dc in next dc, ch 1, * 2 dc in each of next 2 dc, ch 1, rep from * around, join to top of ch-3.

Rnd 3: **Ch 5, work 1 tr loosely in 3rd dc in group of 4 made in previous rnd, ch 4, sl st in top of tr, ch 5, sk next dc, sl st in ch-1 sp, * ch 4, sl st in 4th ch from hook, rep from * 2 times, sl st in same ch-1 sp, rep from ** around, join and end off.

Snowflake 2: (approximately 4¾ inches across)
Starting at center, ch 6, join with sl st to form ring.

Rnd 1: Ch 1, work 12 sc into ring, join.

Rnd 2: Ch 5, * work dc in next sc, ch 2, rep from * around, join to 3rd ch of ch-5.

Rnd 3: Ch 10, sc in 2nd ch from hook, dc in each of next 8 ch [petal made], sl st in next dc, (ch 7, sl st into sp) 2 times, ch 7, sl st in next dc, rep from * around, ending with a ch-4, dc into last sp.

Rnd 4: * Sc in 4th ch and each of next 5 ch along side of petal, sl st in ch at tip of petal, (ch 4, sl st in 4th ch from hook for pc) 3 times, sl st in same st at tip of petal, sc in each of next 6 sts along other side of petal, ch 1, sc into top of first ch-7 lp, ch 1, sc into top of next lp, ch 3, sl st into sc just made, ch 1, sc into next lp, ch 1, rep from * around, join and end off.

Snowflake 3: (approximately 5½ inches across)
Starting at center, ch 4, join with sl st to form ring, ch 3.

Rnd 1: Work 11 dc into ring, join in top of ch-3.

Rnd 2: Ch 3, dc in same st, ch 2, sk 1 dc, * dc in next dc, ch 2, sk 1 dc, rep from * 4 times, join at top of ch-3, ch 3.

Rnd 3: Work 2 dc in next dc, ch 4, * 1 dc in next dc, 2 dc in next dc, ch 4, rep from * around, join, ch 3.

Rnd 4: Work 2 dc in next dc, 1 dc in next dc, ch 5, * dc in next 2 dc, 2 dc in next dc, 1 dc in next dc, ch 5, rep from * around, join.

Rnd 5: * Ch 3, sl st in next dc, ch 5, sl st in 4th ch from hook for pc, ch 2, sl st in next dc, ch 3, sl st in next dc, (ch 6, sl st in 4th ch from hook for pc) 3 times, ch 2, dc into base of 2nd pc from hook, ch 4, sl st into top of dc just made, ch 2, tr into base of next pc, ch 4, sl st into tr just made, ch 2, sl st into next dc, rep from * around. Join and end off.

Snowflake 4: (Use 1 ball of perle cotton #8 in white and a steel #2 hook)
Make a foundation ch of 8, join with sl st.

Rnd 1: Ch 8, * work 1 tr, ch 4 into ring *. Rep bet *'s around. Join with sl st in 4th of ch-8.

Rnd 2: Work 1 sl st in ch-4 lp, ch 3, work 5 dc in same sp. Work 6 dc in all ch-4 lps around. End with sl st.

Rnd 3: Ch 4, 5 tr in next 5 dc's, ch 5, * 1 tr in next 6 dc's, ch 5 *. Rep bet *'s around. Join with sl st.

Rnd 4: Work 1 sl st in 2nd tr, ch 4, 1 tr in next 3 trs joined. * Ch 7, 1 sc in ch-5 lp, ch 7, make 4 joined tr in 2nd, 3rd, 4th, and 5th tr of previous rnd *. Rep bet *'s around. Join with sl st.

Rnd 5: Work 5 sc, 1 pc, 5 sc in ch-7 lp. Rep 15 times. Join with sl st. Fasten off.

Snowflake 5: (Use 1 ball of perle cotton #8 and a #2 steel hook) Make a foundation ch of 16. Join with sl st.

Rnd 1: Work 26 sc in ring. Join with sl st.

Rnd 2: Ch 3, 1 dc in every sc around. Join with sl st.

Rnd 3: Work 1 sc in *and* bet every dc [52 sc]. Join with sl st.

Rnd 4: Ch 6, 1 dtr (i.e., yarn around 3 times) in next 3 sc. Keep last lp of dtr on hook and join tog through all 4 lps on hook. *Ch 7, dtr in next 4 sc joined *. Rep bet *'s around [13 petals and 13 lps]. Join with sl st.

Rnd 5: Work 4 sc, 1 pc (picot = ch 5), insert hook in first ch; yo hook. Draw through st and lp on hook. Work 4 sc in all 13 lps. Fasten off.

Large Snowflake Ornament: (Use 1 ball of perle cotton #8 and a #5 steel hook)
This snowflake pattern makes an ornament that measures 4½ inches across. Once starched it can also be used as a coaster, if desired. In this way your crochet work can be used and displayed all year.

Rnd 1: Make foundation ch of 10. Join with sl st.

Rnd 2: Ch 1, work 15 sc in ring. Join with sl st.

Rnd 3: Ch 5, * work 1 dc in next st, ch 1. Rep from * around. Join with sl st.

Rnd 4: Work 1 sc in each and bet each 2 dc around. Join with sl st.

Rnd 5: * Ch 6, sk 3 sc, 1 sc in next sc, rep 7 times from *.

Rnd 6: Work 9 sc in each sp.

Rnd 7: Sl st in next 4 sts. Ch 3, dc in next 2 sts, * ch 6, dc in 4th, 5th, and 6th sc in next sp. Rep 6 times from *. Ch 6 and join with sl st.

Rnd 8: Sc in each and bet each 2 dc and in all the chs around. Join with sl st.

Rnd 9: Ch 5 and 4 joined tr, ch 7, 1 dtr in 4th sc, * ch 7, 5 joined tr in the 5-sc above the 3 dtr in Rnd 7, ch 7, 1 dtr in the 3rd sc, ch 3, 1 dtr in the 4th sc. Rep from * 6 times, ending with ch-7 and sl st.

Rnd 10: * Work 10 sc on ch-7, 3 sc, ch 5, and join with sl st to first ch, 3 sc, 10 sc in ch-7 sp. Rep from * 7 times more. Join and fasten off.

DIRECTIONS FOR STARCHING AND BLOCKING

1. With waterproof pen, draw the pattern on the typing paper (approximately 6 per sheet) and tape the paper to the Styrofoam sheet. Cover all with plastic wrap and tape in place.

2. Soak snowflakes in stiffening agent; squeeze out excess, blotting between paper towels if necessary.

3. Place snowflakes on pattern, matching centers. Pin outside points along pattern lines. Then repin, stretching opposite points against each other.

4. Finish by pinning each picot and each loop.

5. Allow to dry.

6. Make a loop of fine thread or monofilament line, and tie for hanging.

Doggie Coat

Make a coat to fit your dog's size and color. You can even fit the coat to your puppy's personality, or create a new look for your animal. If you have a black dog and want to see what he or she would look like with spots, make this coat with black and white granny squares. Or arrange a tri-color grouping to suit your Basset Hound.

Materials: Acrylic knitting worsted, 4-ply
yarn—one skein, or 3½ ozs. in colors of
your choice
4 large buttons

Hook: H

Gauge: 1 motif = 4 inches

Sizes:
For tiny dog do 2 rnds
For medium dog do 3 rnds
For large dog do 4 rnds

DIRECTIONS
Make the following number of squares in each color: 8 black, 7 brown, and 4 white.

Ch 7, sl st in first ch to form ring.

Rnd 1: Ch 2 [counts as 1 dc], 2 dc in ring, ch 3. Work (3 dc in ring, ch 3) 3 times, sl st in top of ch-2 at beg of rnd.

Rnd 2: Ch 2, dc in each of next 2 dc, (2 dc, ch 3, 2 dc in corner sp) *dc in each of next 3 dc, (2 dc, ch 3, 2 dc in corner sp), rep from * 3 times. Sl st in top of ch-2.

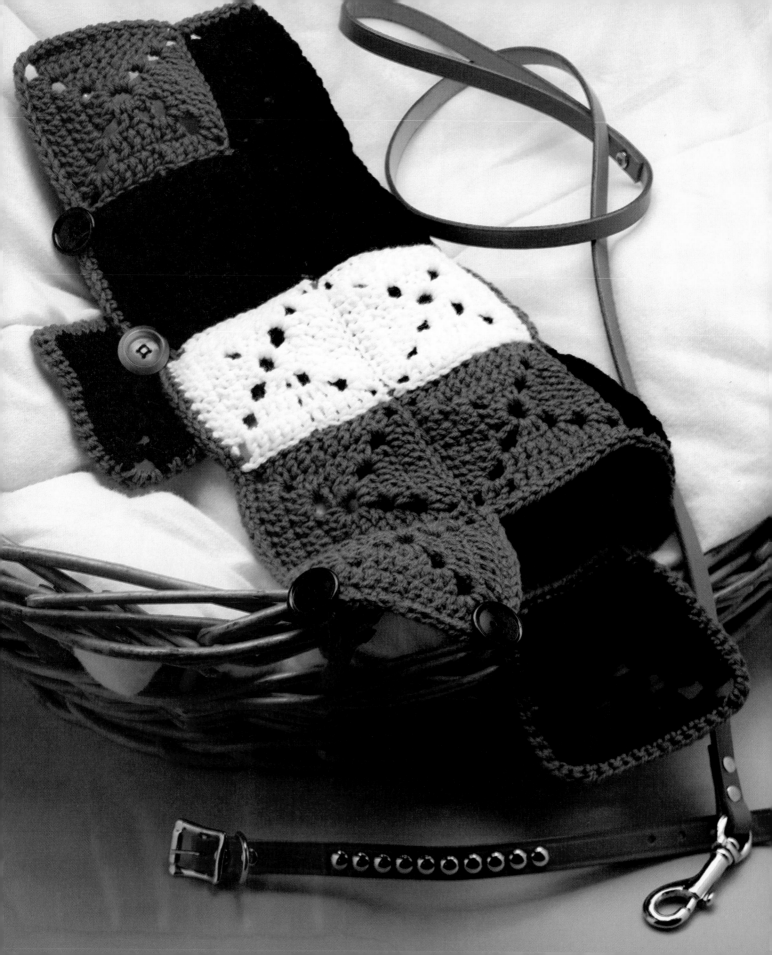

Rnd 3: Ch 2, dc in each of next 4 dc, (2 dc, ch 3, 2 dc in corner sp) *dc in each of next 7 dc, (2 d, ch 3, 2 dc in corner sp), rep from * 3 times, dc in last 2 dc. Sl st in top of ch-2.

Rnd 4: Ch 2, dc in each of next 6 dc, (2 dc, ch 3, 2 dc in corner sp) * dc in each of next 11 dc, (2 dc, ch 3, 2 dc in corner sp), rep from * 3 times. Dc in last 4 dc. Sl st in top of ch-2.

FINISH

Arrange squares as shown in Diagram. Sc squares tog from wrong side, working 1 sc through each pair of corresponding dc, picking up back lps of dc only, and working 1 sc in corner sps.

Work 1 row of sc around entire piece, doing 3 sc in each corner lp. Fasten off.

Attach button to each corner of 1 neck square and to each corner of piece that goes under belly. Use corner spaces as buttonholes for buttons.

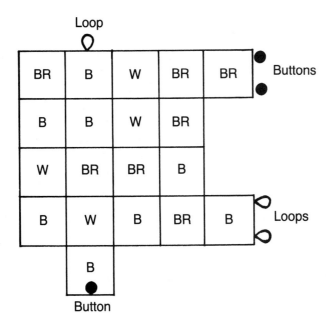

Pretty Note Cards

When you want to make something small and pretty to give as a gift, why not try your hand at making your own greeting cards? Or, if you are having a party, dress up the table with place cards adorned with a little crocheted motif. This is a nice way to send greetings, and your friends will be delighted to have some of your handwork to take home with them or to keep.

Materials: Coats & Clark Speed Cro-Sheen in small amounts of multicolored pastel, or a variety of different colors of perle cotton

Hook: #00 steel

DIRECTIONS

Ch 5 and join into ring with sl st in first ch.

Rnd 1: Ch 1, work 13 sc in ring, sl st to first ch.

Rnd 2: Ch 1, sc in next sc, * ch 4, ** yo 2 times, insert hook into next st, yo, draw lp through, (yo, draw through 2 lps) 2 times **. Rep from ** to ** 2 times more in same st, yo, draw through 4 lps on hook, ch 3, sc into each of next 2 sc, rep from * 3 times more.

Make a ch of 6 for the stem. Turn and work 1 sl st into next sc on flower. Fasten off. Make as many of these as desired. If you want to attach flowers in a cl, make each stem a different length, so that flowers will grow at different heights. Refer to the Basket of Roses on page 37 for another idea for using these designs. You might want to add some leaves, as well. (Directions on page 39).

These little flowers would look nice on barrettes, a small evening purse, mittens, a cap, or down the front of a sweater with buttons in the centers.

Cards

Cut posterboard to desired size to fit flowers. Patterned cards are covered with calico fabric and the center is then cut out for flower placement. Attach to background with white glue.

Flower Appliqué: (Use a scrap of pink sport yarn and a D hook) Ch 6, join to first ch with sl st to form ring.

To make petal: * Ch 6, work sc in 2nd ch from hook, hdc in next ch, dc in next ch, hdc in next ch, sc in next ch. Join with sl st in ring. Rep from * around until you have made 8 petals. Join with sl st. Fasten off.

These flowers can be used for decoration on mittens, caps, note cards, slippers, and more. See mittens on page 151.

Strawberry Appliqué: (Use red and green sport yarn and a D hook) Using red yarn, ch 3, sc in last 2 chs, ch 1, turn.

Row 1: Inc 1 st each end, ch 1, turn. Work until there are 8 sc across row. Work even for 1 more row.

Row 2: Work sc in 3 sc, sl st in next 2 sc, sc in last 3 sc, ch 1, turn.

Row 3: Rep Row 2.

Work 1 row sc around entire strawberry. End off.

To make stem: Join green yarn at top center of strawberry, ch 3, sk 2, 1 sc, ch 3, turn, sc in center. Ch 3, 1 sc in 2nd and 3rd ch, sc in center, ch 3, sk 2, 1 sc on other side of strawberry, ch 3, sc in center, ch 3. Fasten off.

Warm and Pretty Mittens

These knit-look gauntlet-cuff mittens are easy and quick to make. They are perfect for cold winter activities and are designed to fit an adult. Use any color yarn and add a pretty appliqué of strawberries, a shamrock, or flowers. This is a good way to use up scraps of colorful yarn.

Materials: Knitting worsted weight yarn—
    2 ozs. gray
Yarn needle

Hook: H

Gauge:
4 sc = 1 inch
5 rows = 1 inch

DIRECTIONS (make 2)
Ch 2 and, starting in 2nd ch from hook, ch 77.

Row 1: Sc in ch-11 to form front of cuff, sl st in ch-6 for wrist shaping, sc in ch-19 for hand, sl st in ch-4 for top of mitten, sc in ch-19 for back of hand, sl st in ch-6 for back of wrist, sc in ch-11 for back of cuff. Ch 1 and turn.

For following rows, with exception of first and last sc in each row, work in *back lps* only.

Rep Row 1 10 times.

Thumb shaping: Sc in sc-11 of cuff, sl st in 6-sc of wrist, sc in first 7-sc of hand, ch 13 for thumb.

Sk next 28 sc of hand, join to next sc, and sc in last 7-sc of back of hand.

Sl st in 6-sc for wrist, sc in 11-sc of back of cuff. Ch 1 and turn. Continue to work in *back lps*.

First thumb row: Sc in 11-sc of cuff, sl st in 6-sc of wrist, sc in first 7-sc of hand, sc in first 5 of ch for thumb. Sl st in ch-3 sps, sc in last 5 of ch for back of thumb. Sc in last 7-sc of back of hand, sl st in 6-sc for wrist, sc in 11 sc of back of cuff. Ch 1 and turn.

Repeat first thumb row 3 times. Fasten off after the last rep.

FINISH

1. Fold mitten in half and, using yarn needle and matching yarn, sew side seams with neat overcast stitch.

2. Sew thumb seam.

3. To make strawberry appliqués, see page 150. Shamrock directions follow.

Shamrock Appliqué: (Use green sport yarn and a D hook)
Ch 2 and work 8 sc in first ch. Join with sl st and turn.

To make first petal: Ch 3, 4 dc in same sp. Turn.

Rnd 1: Ch 3 [first dc], dc in same sp, 1 dc in each of next 3 dc, 2 dc in last dc, ch 2, and turn.

Rnd 2: Dc in first st, hdc in next st, sl st in next 3 sts, dc, sc in last st. Break off yarn, leaving enough yarn to sew appliqué to mitten.

To make 2nd petal: Sk 1 sc of first row and join yarn in next st. Work in same way as for first petal. Work 2 more petals in same way. Fasten off, leaving enough yarn to sew appliqué to mitten.

FINISH

Using large-eye needle and matching yarn color, secure the appliqué in position on back of mitten hand.

You can add 2 strawberries to each mitten, or a shamrock on each, or you might like to decorate the mittens with the flowers from page 150.

Pixie in Santa's Boot Doll

This 4-inch-high pixie doll makes a darling Christmas tree ornament, and the pixie can be removed for a pocket doll. Add a crochet chain for carrying, attaching to a belt or to use on the end of a key ring. It's even adorable on a teenager's dresser.

Materials: Knitting worsted 4-ply yarn—20
    yds. in red, 2 yds. each in green and
    pink
2 pieces of pipe cleaner, 4 and 7 inches
¾-inch pink wooden bead with hole (some
    come with painted face; if not, use
    markers to make a face)
Small amount of polyfil stuffing
Small amount of brown yarn
Yarn needle

Hook: D

DIRECTIONS

Fold 7-inch pipe cleaner in half and insert V-end into bead hole. This is body and legs.

    Place 4-inch pipe cleaner across body and legs, ½ inch below head, and twist once to secure "arms." Set aside.

Shirt Front

Row 1: Using red yarn, ch 12, work 1 sc in 2nd ch from hook and each ch across [11 sc]. Ch 1 and turn.

Rows 2 and 3: Work 1 sc in each sc. Ch 1 and turn.

Shirt Back

Continue with red yarn.

Row 4: Work 1 sc in each of next 4 sc, ch 3 [neck opening], sk 3 sc, 1 sc in each of next 4 sc. Ch 1 and turn.

Row 5: Work 1 sc in each sc and ch across. Ch 1 and turn [11 sc].

Row 6: Rep Row 2 and fasten off.

Hands: (make 2)
Using pink yarn, join on 1 short end and, working in back lps only, work 4 sc across. Ch 1 and turn.

Row 2: (Draw up a lp on each of next 2 sc) 2 times. Cut yarn, leaving a length for sewing bottom of hand.

Sleeve Ruffles

Using red yarn, work 3 sc in each front lp that you skipped when making hands.

Slip neck opening over bead head. Place small amount of stuffing over ends of each pipe cleaner arm. Stitch "hands" to create a closed, round ball coming out of each ruffled sleeve.

Pants

For first leg, join red yarn on back of shirt in 5th st from your left.

Row 1: Work 1 sc in each of next 5 sc for back of leg. Work under arm and 1 sc in first 5 sc on front for leg front [10 sc]. Ch 1 and turn.

Rows 2–7: Work 1 sc in each sc. Ch 1 and turn each row. Fasten off.

Rep for 2nd leg. Cut yarn, leaving a length for sewing. Sew inside leg seams.

Leg Ruffles

Using red yarn, work 3 sc in front lp of each sc around bottom of each leg. Join and fasten off.

Feet: (make 2)
Join green yarn in skipped back lps of leg ruffle.

Row 1: Work 3 sc in each st around. Ch 1 and turn.

Row 2: Work 1 sc in each sc. Fasten off, leaving a length to sew bottom of foot.

Finish

Using red yarn in yarn needle, run through sts where leg ruffle joins leg and pull tightly to gather. Tie.

Rep at waist and weave all ends to outside.

Hat

Using red yarn, ch 12. Join with sl st for ring.

Rnd 1: Work 1 sc in each ch [12 sc]. Do not join rnds; mark beg of each rnd.

Rnds 2–9: Work 1 sc in each sc. At end of Rnd 9, sl st in each of next 2 sc. Fasten off. Using a strand of red, weave through sts on 2nd rnd. Pull up tightly to gather, and tie. Tuck yarn ends under and fasten off.

Finish

Cut ½-inch strands of brown yarn and glue to the inside edge of hat brim for hair. Glue hat and hair to head.

Santa's Boot: (Use 4-ply yarn—15 yards black, 3 yards white— and a G hook)

To make the sole: Using black yarn, ch 12 for foundation ch.

Rnd 1: Work 7 sc in 2nd ch from hook, 1 sc in each of next 9 ch, 3 sc in last sc. Working on opposite side of the foundation ch, work 1 sc in each of next 9 ch [28 sc]. *Do not join rnds.*

Rnd 2: Work 2 sc in each of next 7 sc, 1 sc in next 21 sc [35 sc].

Rnd 3: Start upper part of boot and work in back lps of this rnd only. (Draw up a lp in each of the next 2 sc, work off as 1 sc) 7 times, 1 sc in each of next 21 sc [28 sc].

Rnd 4: (Draw up a lp in each of next 2 sc, work off as 1 sc) 4 times, 1 sc in each of the next 20 sc [24 sc].

Rnds 5–9: Work 1 sc in each sc. Fasten off yarn at end of Rnd 9 after working sl st in each of next 2 sc to even up.

To make the cuff: Join the white yarn (*work in front lps only on this rnd*), sc around and join. Ch 1.

Rnd 2: Work 1 sc in each sc. Join. Cut yarn. Turn cuff down.

Finish

Hold boot with sole away from you and join black yarn. Work 1 sc under each sk st of Rnd 1. Join and fasten off. Tuck ends in.

Sew pixie inside boot. Add a sc ch to back of boot to hang.

Strawberries on a Rope Sachet

Make a hanging strawberry rope to sweeten a closet or to use as a decoration. Consider making the individual strawberries to fill a basket for a cheerful table decoration. This one, topped with two daisies, was designed by Mary F. Smith. The finished length is 24 inches, and there are seven strawberries.

Materials: Knitting worsted 4-ply yarn—2
   ozs. in red, 1 oz. in green, small amounts
   in white and yellow
Polyfil stuffing
Strawberry oil (optional)
¾-inch plastic ring
Yarn needle

Hook: F

DIRECTIONS

Strawberry: (make 7)
Rnd 1: Using red yarn, ch 2, 6 sc in 2nd ch from hook. Do not join rnds; mark beg of each rnd [6 sc].

Rnd 2: *Work 2 sc in next sc, 1 sc in next sc. Rep from * around [9 sc].

Rnd 3: Sc around.

Rnd 4: * Work 2 sc in next sc, 1 sc in next sc. Rep from * around, ending with 2 sc in last sc [14 sc].

Rnd 5: Rep Rnd 3.

Rnd 6: Rep Rnd 2 [21 sc].

Rnds 7–9: Rep Rnd 3.

Rnd 10: * Work 1 sc in each of next 5 sc, pull up a lp in each of next 2 sc, work off as 1 sc [dec made], rep from * around [18 sc].

Rnd 11: * Work sc in each of next 7 sc. Pull up a lp in each of next 2 sc and work off as 1 sc. Rep from * once [16 sc]. Stuff. Add strawberry-scented oil.

Rnd 12: (Pull up a lp in each of next 4 sc and work off as 1 sc) 4 times. Join and fasten off.

Seeds
Separate white 4-ply yarn strands and, using 2 strands, make French knots at random on strawberries for seeds.

Hull: (make 7)
Row 1: Using green yarn, ch 9, sl st in 2nd ch from hook, 1 sc in each of next 2 ch, 1 hdc in each of next 5 ch [8 sts].

Rep Row 1 4 times and join in first ch. Fasten off yarn, leaving a length for sewing to strawberry. Using yarn needle and matching color, make a few sts across the top to close.

Leaves: (make 3)
Row 1: Using green yarn, ch 9, sl st in 2nd ch from hook, sc in next ch, hdc in next ch, 1 dc in each of next 4 dc, 4 dc in last ch on opposite side of foundation ch, 1 dc in each of next 4 ch, hdc in next ch, sc in next ch, sl st in last ch. Fasten off and tuck ends under.

Flower: (make 2)
Using white yarn, ch 5. Join with sl st into ring. * Work 1 sl st, 1 dc, 1 tr, 1 dc, 1 sl st in ring [petal made].

Rep from * 4 times more. Fasten off.

FINISH
Cover plastic ring with sc, using green yarn. Join, but do not cut yarn. Ch 20, sc in top of strawberry. Fasten off.

Join remaining 6 strawberries in following way:

1. Join green yarn in same sc as ch-20 on ring, ch 40, sc in top of next strawberry. Fasten off.

2. Join and end same as Step 1, ch 60.

3. Join and end same as Step 1, ch 60.

4. Join and end same as Step 1, ch 80.

5. Join and end same as Step 1, ch 100.

6. Join and end same as Step 1, ch 110.

Sew 3 leaves together so they are joined at the wide bases with points free. Attach 2 flowers to 2 side leaves with yellow French knots in each center. Attach leaves and flowers to bottom of ring and hang.

Loopy Puppy

Can you imagine the delight of any child when you present him or her with this cuddly puppy made of loops of yarn? You can make several in different colors, and this is a good way to make use of all that leftover yarn from other projects. It is a great bazaar item that is sure to be irresistible.

Materials: Knitting worsted (4-oz. skein) in
  desired color
18 inches of ½-inch-wide satin ribbon
3 shoe buttons (or similar size buttons) for
  eyes and nose
Carpet thread
Small scrap of red felt for tongue
Approximately 3-inch-long piece of cardboard ¾ inches wide
Polyfil stuffing

Hook: H

DIRECTIONS

Double Loop Stitch (db lp st) Pattern
Pull up yarn in st to make 2 lps on hook, * wrap yarn around cardboard and pull through the same st (3 lps on hook), yo and through first lp on hook [there will be 3 lps on hook]. Rep from * once in same st, yo and through all 4 lps on hook. [Each db lp st is an inc st.]

Single Loop Stitch (lp st) Pattern
Work as above, omitting the rep.

Head and Body
Starting at top of head, ch 5; join with sl st.

Rnd 1: Make 6 db lp sts in ring. Do not join rnds. Carry a piece of contrasting color yarn bet first and last sts to mark beg of rnds.

Rnds 2 and 3: Inc 6 db lp sts evenly spaced in each rnd [18 db lp sts in Rnd 3].

Rnds 4–15: Work even on 18 db lp sts.

Rnd 16: Working in sc, * sc in first db lp st, dec over next 2 db lp sts. Rep from * around [12 sc]. Stuff head and body firmly before opening becomes too small.

Rnd 17: * Dec over first 2 sc. Rep from * around [6 sc]. End off, leaving a 12-inch length of yarn for sewing; draw remaining 6 sts tight.

Legs: (make 4)
Beg with a ch-2.

Rnd 1: Work 8 sc in 2nd ch. Do not join rnds. Mark as for head and body.

Rnd 2: (Work in back lps only.) Work even on 8 sc.

Rnds 3 and 4: Work even on 8 sc. End off at end of Rnd 4, leaving a 12-inch length of yarn for sewing.

Tail
Beg with a ch-2.

Rnd 1: Make 6 single lp sts in 2nd ch. Do not join rnds. Mark as for head and body.

Rnds 2–4: Work even on 6 single lp sts. End off at end of Rnd 4, leaving a 12-inch length of yarn for sewing.

Ears: (make 2)
Beg with a ch-5.

Rnd 1: Make a single lp st in 2nd ch from hook and in each of next 2 chs. Make 3 single lp sts in last ch. Working on other side of ch, make a single lp st in each of 3 ch sps and 3 single lp sts in last ch sp.

Next rnd: Make single lp sts in each of first 4 sps, 3 single lp sts in tip of ear, single lp sts in each of the next 4 sps. End off, leaving a 12-inch length of yarn for sewing.

FINISH

Sew ears to either side of head. Stuff legs and sew to the front of body, approximately 4 inches down from the top of head, for front paws and at the bottom of body for rear paws.

Stuff tail and sew to the rear of body. Sew shoe buttons on face for eyes and nose. Cut a tongue from the scrap of red felt and sew to face underneath nose button. Tie a length of ribbon around neck and make a bow on side.

Source List

If you have any trouble obtaining the yarns specified for the projects, you can write to the following addresses for information on mail-order sources or for the name of a store in your area that carries the material.

If you have any problems, suggestions, or experiences to share concerning your craft work, drop me a note at the studio in Nantucket.

Leslie Linsley
Nantucket, MA 02554

Bernat Yarn and Craft Corp.
Uxbridge, MA 01569

Coats & Clark, Inc.
Cummings Point Rd.
Stamford, CT 06902

Caron International Inc.
Avenue E
Rochelle, IL 61068

Phildar, Inc.
6438 Dawson Blvd.
Norcross, GA 30093

Stif'n Fab
Posi Bendr
P.O. Box 2173
Westminster, CA 92683

Tahki Imports Ltd.
92 Kennedy St.
Hackensack, NJ 07601

William Unger & Company Inc.
230 Fifth Ave.
New York, NY 10011

Mail Order for Phildar Yarns
Creative Needles
436 Ave. of the Americas
New York, NY 10011

Mail Order Patterns
Anne Lane Originals
P.O. Box 206
North Abington, MA 02351

Sally V. George
The Crochet Works
1472 Auburn
Baker, OR 97814